KINGFISHER
RIDING CLUB

HORSES &PONIES

WRITTEN BY
Sandy Ransford

PHOTOGRAPHED BY
Bob Langrish

KING*f*ISHER

NEW YORK

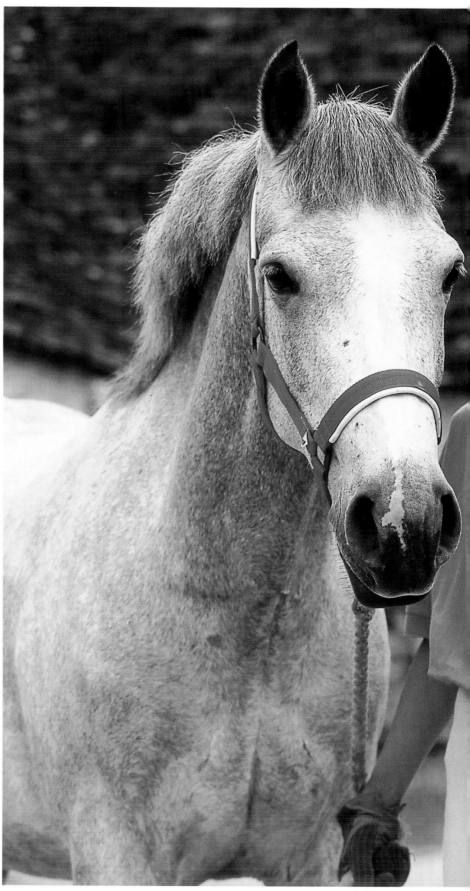

KINGFISHER

Larousse Kingfisher Chambers Inc.
80 Maiden Lane
New York, New York 10038
www.kingfisherpub.com

First published in 2001
3 5 7 9 10 8 6 4

3TR/1101/TWP/MAR/ARM130

LIBRARY OF CONGRESS
CATALOGING-IN-PUBLICATION DATA
Ransford, Sandy.
   Horses & ponies/by Sandy Ransford.—
1st ed.
      p. cm.— (Kingfisher riding club)
   ISBN 0-7534-5343-6
      1. Horses—Juvenile literature. 2.
Ponies—Juvenile literature. 3. Horse
breeds—Juvenile literature. [1. Horses. 2.
Ponies. 3. Horse breeds.] I. Title: Horses
and ponies. II. Title. III. Series.

SF302 .R35 2001
798.2'3—dc21   00-047903

Designed and edited by
BOOKWORK
Editor: Louise Pritchard
Art Director: Jill Plank
Assistant Editor: Annabel Blackledge
Designer: Yolanda Carter

For Kingfisher:
Managing Editor: Miranda Smith
Managing Art Director: Mike Davis
DTP Coordinator: Nicky Studdart
Consultant: Lesley Ward
Coordinating Editor: Denise Heal

Printed in Singapore

*Kingfisher would like to thank The Talland School
of Equitation, Gloucestershire, England, for their
invaluable help in the production of this book.*

Contents

Presenting horses and ponies

Croup

Point of hip

Loin

Dock

Flank

Stifle

Tail

Thigh

Gaskin (second thigh)

Point of hock

Hock

Tendons

Ergot (small lump on the back of the fetlock joint)

Horses, ponies, wild asses, and zebras all belong to the horse family. They are descended from the same ancestors, but they have evolved differently. All domestic horses and ponies, from the largest Shire horse to the tiniest miniature pony, are the same species. Ponies are smaller than horses and more mischievous.

Przewalski's horse
This species of wild horse was discovered in Mongolia in 1881. It looks like the wild ancestors of modern domestic horses and ponies.

Points of a horse

It is useful to know the names and positions of all the points of a horse or pony. It will help you understand the instructions you are given when you learn to ride and look after a pony. The picture above shows the basic points—there are many more.

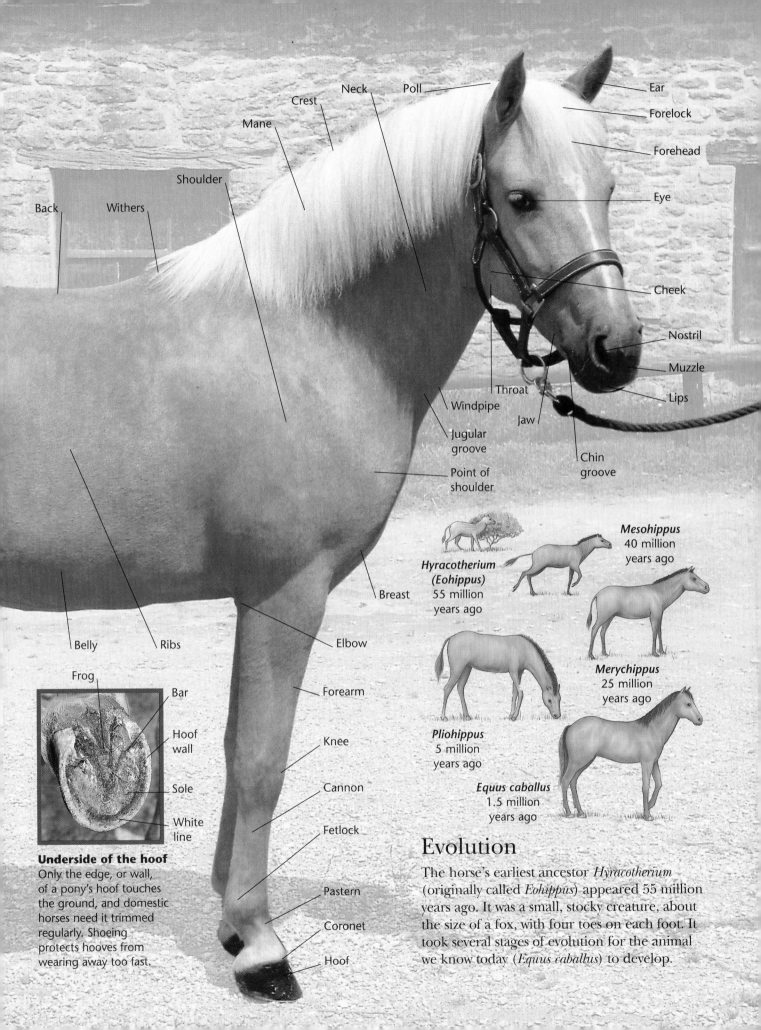

Back

Withers

Shoulder

Mane

Crest

Neck

Poll

Ear

Forelock

Forehead

Eye

Cheek

Nostril

Muzzle

Throat

Lips

Windpipe

Jaw

Jugular
groove

Chin
groove

Point of
shoulder

Breast

Belly

Ribs

Elbow

Frog

Bar

Hoof
wall

Sole

White
line

Forearm

Knee

Cannon

Fetlock

Pastern

Coronet

Hoof

Underside of the hoof
Only the edge, or wall,
of a pony's hoof touches
the ground, and domestic
horses need it trimmed
regularly. Shoeing
protects hooves from
wearing away too fast.

Mesohippus
40 million
years ago

*Hyracotherium
(Eohippus)*
55 million
years ago

Merychippus
25 million
years ago

Pliohippus
5 million
years ago

Equus caballus
1.5 million
years ago

Evolution

The horse's earliest ancestor *Hyracotherium*
(originally called *Eohippus*) appeared 55 million
years ago. It was a small, stocky creature, about
the size of a fox, with four toes on each foot. It
took several stages of evolution for the animal
we know today (*Equus caballus*) to develop.

Natural world of horses

Horses and ponies are herd animals. They form small groups, and within the groups there are particular friendships and sometimes dislikes. In the wild, horses spend up to 20 hours a day grazing, roaming freely in search of food. When they rest, at least one group member stands guard over its sleeping companions.

Domesticated horses

A pony can feel unhappy if it is kept on its own. If there are no other horses or ponies around, other animals, like sheep and cows, make good company. The life of a domesticated pony is not natural, so try to give your pony as much freedom as possible.

Mutual grooming

Wild and domesticated ponies often groom each other if they are friends. They scratch each other's necks, withers, or backs with their front teeth. This is their way of strengthening a friendship.

Flehmen reaction

A pony may curl up its top lip when it senses an unusual smell or taste. This strange action lets it draw air over special sense organs in the roof of its mouth, so that it can analyze the smell.

A horse's body language

Ears pricked forward show that a horse is interested in what is going on and expects good things to happen.

One ear to the side shows that the pony is distracted by something other than his main object of interest.

Ears laid back show anger or fear. The pony is warning you, or another pony, that it may kick or bite.

Herd animals

In the wild, horses and ponies, such as these mustangs, live in small family groups. These groups consist of one stallion, a few mares and their foals, and young animals that stay until they form herds of their own.

Fighting talk

In a group of horses and ponies, each animal has a position in a hierarchy, and squabbles occur if one horse tries to challenge for a higher position. In the wild, stallions fight off rivals, biting and striking out with a foreleg, or swinging their hindquarters around, ready to kick. But horses and ponies threaten each other much more than they actually fight. Usually, ears laid back and an outstretched neck are enough to frighten away another pony.

Colors and markings

There are many variations in the colors of horses and ponies, but most are a shade of brown or gray and have dark skin. Some horses and ponies change color as they age. Most "white" ponies were originally gray, but have become paler in color with maturity. Completely black horses are rare.

Colors

Even within the color groups there are different shades. Bays can be lighter or darker; grays vary from almost black to white. A pony's coat is described as white only if it has pink skin.

Dapple gray
Gray and black hairs forming clear rings

Pinto
Black (or brown) and white areas all over

Palomino
Golden with a pale, often white, mane and tail

Bay
Dark brown with black mane, tail, and legs

Chestnut and Sorrel
Red-gold all over (mane and tail, too)

Bay mare and foal
This mare is a bay. She has a rich brown coat and black "points"—that is, a black mane, tail, and lower legs.

Striped
This chestnut pony has a stripe on its face and two white socks.

Appaloosa

The Appaloosa is a registered breed of horse known for its spotted coat. It has either a light coat with dark spots, or a dark coat with light spots. Some Appaloosas can be a solid color, but they may have mottled skin or striped hooves.

Head markings

Some ponies have white markings on their faces. A mark down the face is a stripe. A broad stripe is a blaze. Some ponies have white faces—sometimes called a "bald" face.

Bald face   Stripe

Leg markings

White coronet

White pastern

White fetlock

White cannon

A white band above the hoof is called a white coronet. A white pastern or fetlock is often called a sock. A white area reaching up the cannon to the knee or hock is often called a stocking.

A horse's age

You can tell how old a horse is by looking at its teeth. As it ages, the horse's incisors (front teeth) slope more, and their surface markings change.

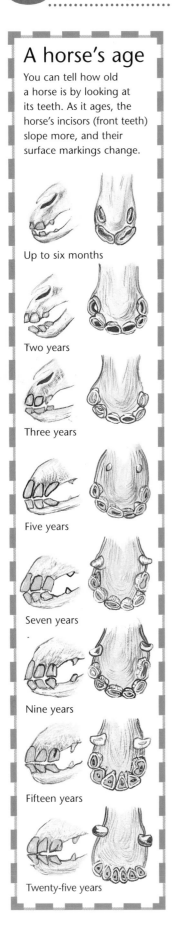

Up to six months

Two years

Three years

Five years

Seven years

Nine years

Fifteen years

Twenty-five years

Learning more about horses

The more you get to know about horses and ponies, the more you will realize how much there is to learn. And if you own your own pony, you owe it to your pony to learn as much as you can. When you know how a healthy horse or pony should look and behave, you will be able to notice signs of illness or lameness in your own pony.

Measuring up

A horse is measured from the top of its withers to the ground. You can use a measuring stick with a horizontal bar that rests on the withers. Usually, horses and ponies are measured in "hands." There are 4 inches (10cm) in a hand— about the width of an adult's hand. Today, height is also given in feet and inches or in meters and centimeters.

What is normal for your pony?

Although the general signs of good and bad health are the same for all horses and ponies, some may behave slightly differently. For example, it may seem odd for a pony to be lying down during the day, but some ponies like to have a nap around mid-morning. Get to know what is normal for your pony.

Senses

Like you, horses and ponies have five senses, but theirs are much more acute than yours. Your pony's wild ancestors were preyed on by wolves and other carnivores. Their finely tuned senses protected them in the wild by warning them when danger was near.

Sight
A horse's prominent eyes allow it to see behind, to the side, and in front.

Smell and taste
A horse's sense of smell is especially acute. It can even smell if a stranger is approaching.

Hearing
A horse's ears are very mobile—they can turn in the direction of a sound quickly.

Touch
If a fly lands on a horse's skin, it can twitch the exact muscle to make the fly move.

Fit for anything

Healthy horses and ponies are alert and interested in everything going on around them. They have bright, clear eyes and they never have runny eyes or noses. They have shiny coats and always show great interest in their food.

Horse breeds

For thousands of years, people have bred horses for specific purposes—heavy draft horses for pulling a plow, hardy ones for herding cattle, or fast horses for racing. Now that people no longer use horses as their primary form of transportation, they breed them for racing or eventing. As needs and demands change, new breeds continue to be created.

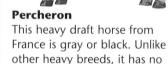

Palomino
Usually a Quarter Horse, this color breed is distinguished by its golden coat and white or cream mane and tail.

Arabian
The oldest horse breed, the Arabian is famed for its beauty and stamina.

Lipizzaner
This strong horse is famous for its use by the Spanish Riding School in Vienna.

Thoroughbred
Descended from the Arabian, this fast horse is used for racing.

Percheron
This heavy draft horse from France is gray or black. Unlike other heavy breeds, it has no long hair, or feathers, on its legs.

Andalusian
Descended from the Spanish horse and the Barb from northern Africa, the Andalusian is usually bay or gray with a long, wavy mane and tail. It has beautiful gaits. The famous Lipizzaners were bred from Andalusians in the 1500s.

American Quarter Horse

The Quarter Horse is the first all-American breed. It got its name because it was bred to race short distances—no more than a quarter of a mile. It is fast and nimble and has a good temperament, so it is ideal for ranch work.

Australian Stock Horse

The Australian Stock Horse was bred for work on Australia's cattle and sheep stations. It was developed in the 1800s from the Thoroughbred and the Waler. Easy to handle, it is a good all-round horse with great stamina.

❶ Selle Français
This French horse was bred for athletic ability—it does well in jumping and eventing.

❷ Waler
The name is a short form of New South Wales in Australia. This horse excels at jumping.

❸ Akhal-Teke
From Turkmenistan, in northern Asia, this breed is often a golden color.

❹ American Saddlebred
This flashy, showy breed performs special gaits. Horses can be three- or five-gaited.

❺ Morgan
Morgans are descended from Justin Morgan, a stallion foaled in Massachusetts in 1793.

❻ Standardbred
The Standardbred is a harness-racing horse. Some horses race at a trot, but others "pace," which means they move their legs on the same side together, instead of moving diagonally.

❼ Trakehner
A tall, East Prussian horse, the Trakehner is excellent at jumping and dressage.

Pony breeds

A pony is no more than 14.2 hands (58 in./147cm) high. There are many different breeds of ponies in the world. Some, like the native breeds of Britain, have existed for thousands of years in a semiwild state. Others, like the Pony of the Americas, have only been around since the 1950s. Most ponies are not purebred.

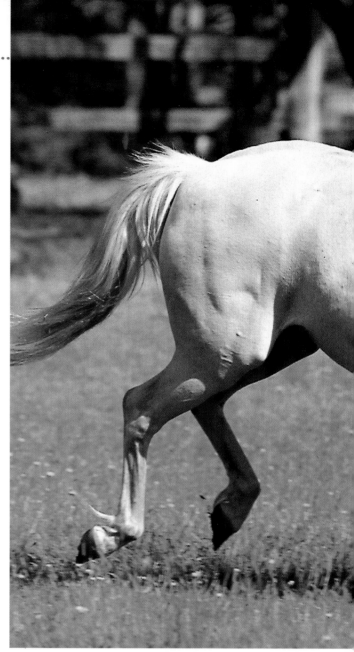

Icelandic horse
Descended from Norwegian and Scottish island ponies, the Icelandic horse has existed for over 1,000 years, and it was once Iceland's main form of transportation. Although it is small—12–13 hands (52 in./122–132cm)—it is usually called a horse, and it is very strong and hardy.

Welsh Pony
There are four breeds of Welsh ponies, ranging from the largest, the Welsh Cob, to the smallest, the Welsh Mountain Pony. In between are the Welsh Pony and the Welsh Pony of Cob Type. This mare with her foal is a Welsh Mountain Pony.

Australian Pony

Recognized as a breed since the 1920s, the Australian Pony was developed from several imported breeds, notably the Welsh Mountain Pony, which it resembles. It has good conformation (a balanced build) and is a good-quality riding pony.

Chincoteague

Chincoteague ponies are some of the last truly wild ponies in the world. They live on islands off the coasts of Maryland and Virginia and may be the descendants of shipwrecked horses from north Africa that swam ashore in the 1500s.

American Shetland

Bred in the 1900s, largely from Hackney ponies, the American Shetland has a narrow build compared to its Scottish ancestors. It is a popular harness pony.

❶ Highland
The Highland, from Scotland, is often gray or dun. It is a popular trekking pony.

❷ Dales
Black, bay, or brown, the Dales is a driving pony originally from northern England.

❸ New Forest Pony
The New Forest Pony is a popular riding pony that originates from southern England.

❹ Connemara
The only native Irish pony, the Connemara is tough and athletic. It is often gray.

❺ Fjord
Cream or dun in color, with a dark dorsal stripe, the Fjord comes from Norway.

❻ Fell
Always black or brown, the Fell comes from northern England. It is a popular driving pony.

❼ Dartmoor
An excellent riding pony from southwest England, the Dartmoor is a good jumper.

❽ Haflinger
Chestnut or palomino, the Haflinger is a strong riding or driving pony from Austria.

❾ Shetland
Stocky and extremely strong, this tiny pony is from the Shetland Islands, off Scotland.

❿ Caspian
The Caspian comes from the Arabian Peninsula. It is fast and a skillful jumper.

Bridles and other tack

Tack is the name for the riding equipment that you use on a horse or pony, including the bridle and bit, saddle, girth, stirrups, and martingale.

A bridle's name—for example, snaffle or double—refers to its bit. Ponies usually wear a snaffle bridle. Bridles are made in different sizes, and you can buy parts separately. Each bit design works in a slightly different way and suits different horses and ponies.

Snaffle bridle

Western bridle
This western bridle has a split-ear crownpiece that fits around the ears. Western bridles do not have a noseband—this horse has a tie down, which is like a standing martingale. Some western bridles are bitless. Others have only a curb bit.

Western tack

Western tack is similar to that used by cowboys, whose horses are trained to respond to the slightest touch on the reins. To stop their saddles from slipping, the horses wear breastplates. These attach to a D ring at the front of the saddle.

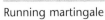

Running martingale

Standing martingale

Martingales

A martingale is designed to stop a horse or pony from tossing its head. It consists of a long strap that fastens around the girth at one end. A standing martingale buckles around the noseband, and a running martingale divides into two straps ending in rings, through which the reins pass. Both kinds of martingales are held in place by a neck strap.

Snaffle bridle

The simplest bridle is called a snaffle bridle. Different nosebands and bits can be attached to it. The cavesson noseband and snaffle bit are used most often.

Crownpiece

Browband

Cavesson noseband

Cheekpiece

Throatlash

Flash noseband

Eggbutt snaffle bit

Reins

Double bridle
This bridle has two bits—a snaffle called a bridoon, and a curb bit called a Weymouth. This type of bridle is usually used for dressage.

Jointed eggbutt snaffle

Loose-ring snaffle

Straight bar rubber snaffle

French-link snaffle

Kimberwick curb bit

Pelham

Bits

An eggbutt snaffle is designed to stop the rings from pinching the corners of a horse's mouth. Pelhams and Kimberwicks are types of curb bits. The curb chain rests in the groove of the horse's chin. When pressure is put on the reins, the chain tightens, giving the rider more control.

Flash noseband
Named after a horse called Flash that wore one, this kind of noseband is attached to the front of a cavesson. It fastens under the bit and helps to keep a horse or pony's mouth shut.

Girths

The saddle is held in place by a girth, which is buckled to the billets under the saddle flap. Girths are made of leather, webbing, or synthetic material. Some, such as a shaped girth, are specifically designed to avoid rubbing the pony's elbows.

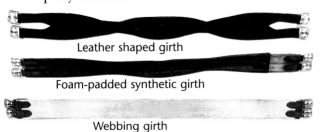

Leather shaped girth

Foam-padded synthetic girth

Webbing girth

Types of saddles

Saddles are made on a rigid framework called a tree, which is made of wood and metal, or sometimes fiberglass. Traditionally the seat is made of pigskin, although sometimes other leathers are used. Nowadays, some saddles are made from synthetic materials, which are cheaper. There are many kinds of saddles, shaped according to their intended use—general riding, jumping, dressage, or showing.

Saddle flap

Knee roll

Buckle guard

Billets

Sweat flap

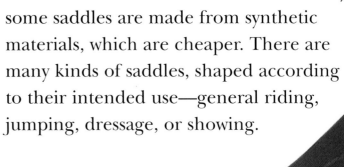

The basic English saddle

A general purpose saddle is suitable for most types of riding. It has forward-cut flaps and slight knee rolls to prevent your knees from sliding forward when jumping. You can use the saddle equally well for trail rides, for an equitation class at a local show, and for dressage at novice level.

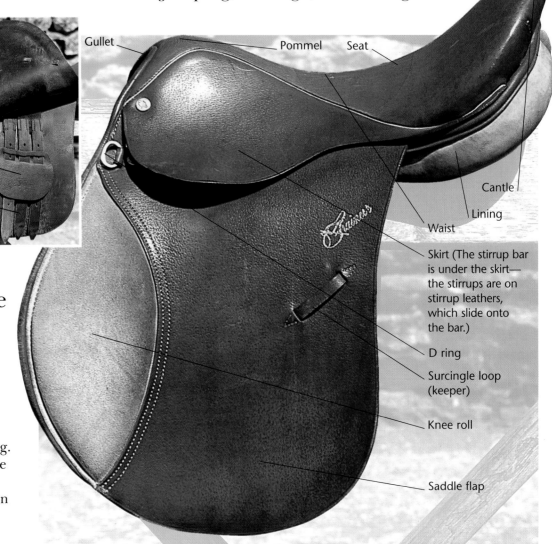

Gullet

Pommel

Seat

Cantle

Lining

Waist

Skirt (The stirrup bar is under the skirt—the stirrups are on stirrup leathers, which slide onto the bar.)

D ring

Surcingle loop (keeper)

Knee roll

Saddle flap

Dressage saddle

The dressage saddle is designed to help you sit deep in the seat in a long leg position. It has straight flaps to show off the horse's shoulder.

Cleaning tack

You should clean your tack every time you use it. Clean, supple leather will not crack, break, or rub the pony. When you clean it, check the stitching to make sure that nothing needs repairing.

First, wash the bit. Clean the oil and dirt off the bridle, saddle, and stirrup leathers with a damp cloth, then rub with saddle soap all over, working it in well. Do not get the sponge too wet, because water is bad for the leather.

Cleaning the bridle on a hanging hook

Cleaning the saddle on a saddle horse

Knee rolls
Large knee rolls support your knee comfortably when you take a jumping position.

Forward-seat jumping saddle

The forward-seat jumping saddle is designed for use with shorter stirrup leathers. It is shaped to help you sit correctly in a jumping position and maintain your balance. It has pronounced forward-cut flaps and large knee rolls, and may have a deep seat.

Western saddle

The western saddle was originally designed for cowboys, who tied roped steers to the high horn at the front. It has wooden stirrups covered with leather, which are comfortable for the feet. Cowboys lived in their saddle, spending hours riding, so the saddle carried all they needed.

Sidesaddle

For 600 years, up until the early 1900s, women rode sidesaddle. Today, you usually see sidesaddle riding only in the show ring. The rider's legs fit around two pommels. She controls the near side of the horse with her left leg, and the off side with a long whip.

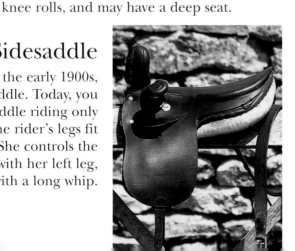

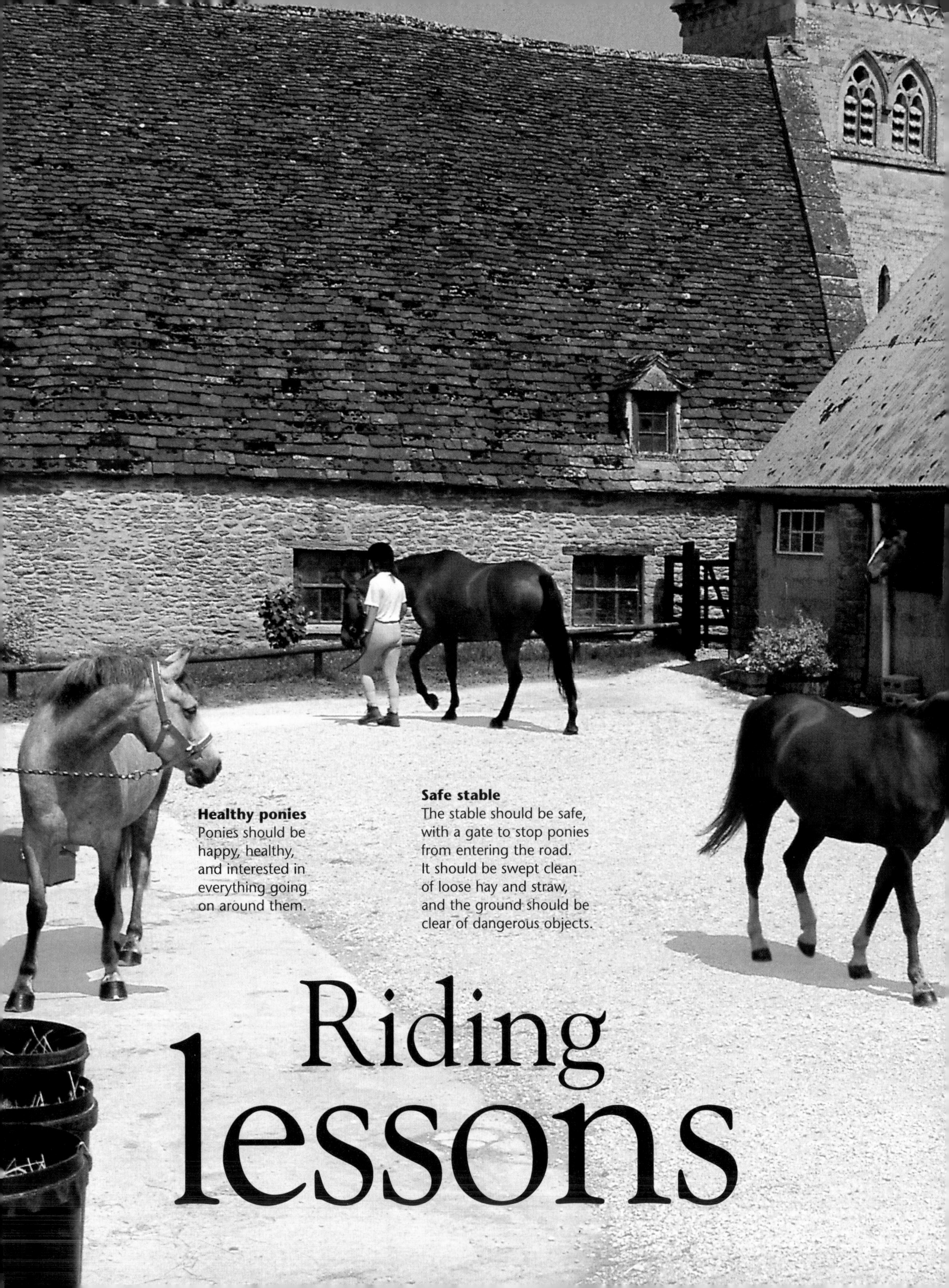

Healthy ponies
Ponies should be
happy, healthy,
and interested in
everything going
on around them.

Safe stable
The stable should be safe,
with a gate to stop ponies
from entering the road.
It should be swept clean
of loose hay and straw,
and the ground should be
clear of dangerous objects.

Riding
lessons

Tidy tack room
For the safety of riders and the comfort of ponies, tack must be looked after properly and stored neatly.

Experienced staff
The staff and helpers should know how to handle the horses and ponies safely and quietly. They should be friendly and helpful.

Happy clients
Observe other children learning to ride. See if they are enjoying themselves.

When you decide to learn to ride, it is important to choose a good stable. If possible, visit more than one before you arrange a lesson. Have a good look around, and find out if it has a riding school that provides lessons. The horses and ponies should look well fed, clean, and content. All of the stalls should be clean and the stable and tack room well organized.

Hunt cap

Tie (for boys)

Show jacket

Riding clothes

Riding wear used to be formal, but today, outside the show ring, you can wear more casual clothes. The one essential is a helmet with a chinstrap. This can be either a schooling helmet or a velvet-covered hunt cap. You can wear a sturdy, heeled boot, but short paddock boots (ankle length) or tall riding boots (knee length) are more comfortable and safer. Jodhpurs or breeches are more comfortable than jeans.

Looking the part

Whether you wear formal or casual clothes while you are riding, it is always practical for safety and comfort to tuck in your shirt and to tie back long hair.

Breeches

Nonslip gloves

Cool cotton shirt (long- or short-sleeved)

Jodhpurs

Tall boots

Jodhpur boots

Casual
Without a tie and jacket, you will feel more comfortable when having lessons or riding for fun.

Formal
Formal wear is usually necessary for dressage and show jumping events.

Stay warm

In wet weather, a full-length raincoat will keep you dry. Special straps will stop it from blowing off your legs. Gloves will stop the reins from slipping out of your hands.

In cold weather, wear leggings under jodhpurs.

Wet weather gear

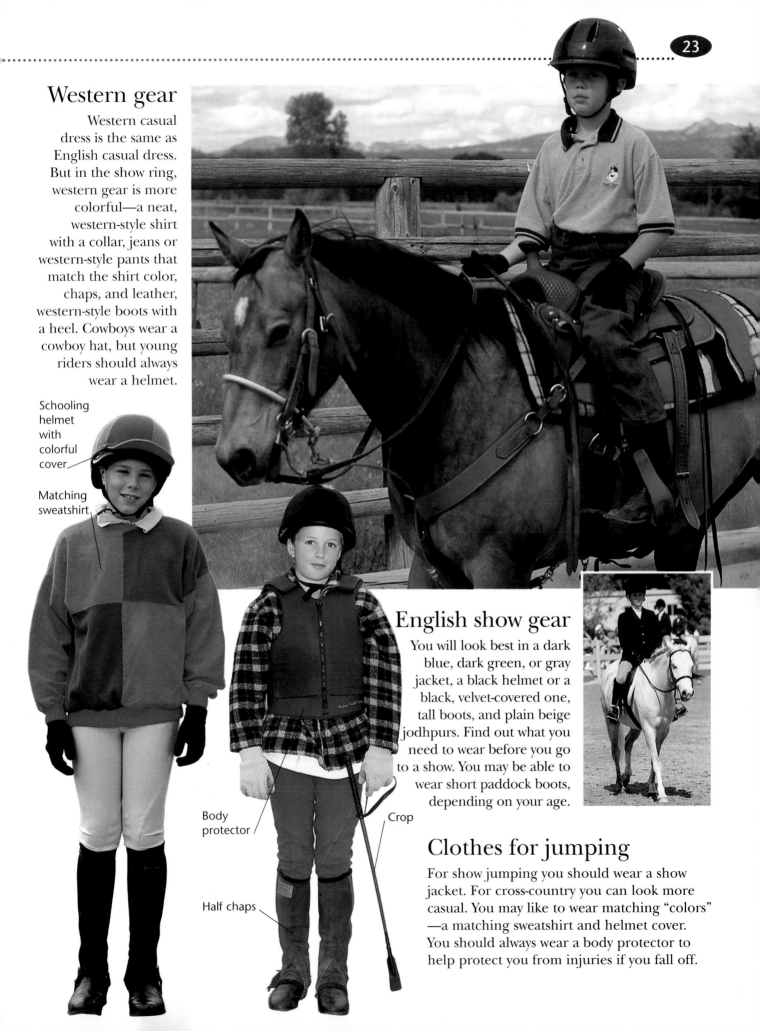

Western gear

Western casual dress is the same as English casual dress. But in the show ring, western gear is more colorful—a neat, western-style shirt with a collar, jeans or western-style pants that match the shirt color, chaps, and leather, western-style boots with a heel. Cowboys wear a cowboy hat, but young riders should always wear a helmet.

Schooling helmet with colorful cover

Matching sweatshirt

Body protector

Crop

Half chaps

English show gear

You will look best in a dark blue, dark green, or gray jacket, a black helmet or a black, velvet-covered one, tall boots, and plain beige jodhpurs. Find out what you need to wear before you go to a show. You may be able to wear short paddock boots, depending on your age.

Clothes for jumping

For show jumping you should wear a show jacket. For cross-country you can look more casual. You may like to wear matching "colors" —a matching sweatshirt and helmet cover. You should always wear a body protector to help protect you from injuries if you fall off.

First meeting

At first, getting to know a horse or pony can be intimidating, but there is nothing to be afraid of. Most ponies are very gentle, but can be nervous. Move slowly and quietly; do not shout or wave your arms. Meeting a new pony is like meeting a stranger. If you walk up to them quietly and confidently, and say something friendly, they will immediately feel at ease.

Introducing yourself

Approach a pony from the front and slightly to the side, walking toward its head so it can get a good look at you. Talk to it so that it can hear you and knows you are a friend. When you get close, let it smell your hand, then pat it on the neck and show it that you are not frightened of it.

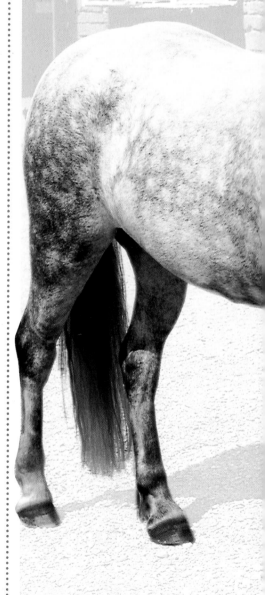

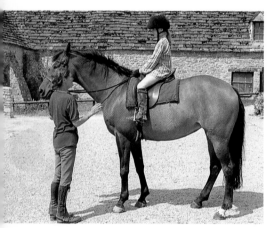

Horse too large
This horse is too large for the rider. The girl's lower legs are in contact with the saddle flaps instead of the horse's sides.

Pony too small
This pony is too small for the rider. The girl's legs are not in contact with the pony, and she may be too heavy for it.

The right size

Your instructor should give you a pony to ride that is the right size for you. When you are sitting correctly in the saddle, the soles of your feet should be level with the line of the pony's tummy. You will then be able to have your legs in the right location, just behind the pony's girth.

Handling ponies

Walk, do not run around the stable and paddock when ponies are around.

Never lose your temper around a pony or get angry or flustered. Try to stay calm around ponies.

Speak quietly to ponies and to friends. Do not shout or shriek with laughter.

Walk up to a pony confidently. Do not be nervous, or you will make it nervous.

Give a pony a pat, or stroke its neck firmly, so you don't tickle it.

Talk to ponies in a firm, friendly way, as if you are used to telling them what to do.

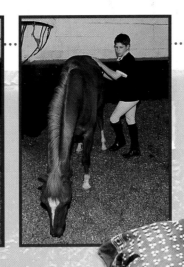

In the stall

Always let your pony know where you are, so you do not startle it. Try to avoid walking behind your pony, but if you have to, speak to it, put a hand on its hindquarters, and slide it down its tail as you go around. This will stop your pony from moving backward. Never walk behind a pony you do not know!

Offering food
Hold your hand out flat with the food on it. Keep your thumb out of the way so that the pony does not bite it by mistake.

Making friends
Listen to what the instructor tells you, and do what she says. You will soon make friends with the pony.

Slip the noseband on
Standing on the pony's left, or near, side, put your right arm under its chin, and slip on the noseband.

Buckle up
Gently flick the crownpiece over the pony's head with your right hand. Hold the cheekpiece in your left hand, reach for the crownpiece with your right hand, and fasten the buckle.

Putting on a halter

You will use a halter to lead a pony from place to place and to tie it up. Most ponies do not mind having a halter put on, but if you have to catch one that is difficult, it may help if you hold out a treat while you slip on the noseband.

Getting ready

Once you become comfortable around a horse or pony, there is still a lot to do before you can get on it and ride. You may have to go out to the paddock and catch your pony before leading it to the stable. Then you can give it a good grooming. When the pony is clean and ready, you will have to tack it up—that is, put on its saddle and bridle. Always give your pony plenty of time to digest its food before you ride it.

Leading a pony

It is traditional to lead a pony on the left-hand side. This is called the near side. (The other side is called the off side.) Hold the lead rope with your right hand near the pony's head and your left hand near the end of the rope.

If the pony acts up, you can let go with your right hand while keeping hold with the left. Don't wind the rope around your left hand. If your pony runs off, your hand could get caught.

When you lead a pony, walk by its shoulder and watch where you are going. Do not walk ahead of the pony, and do not pull it along. When you want to turn, always direct the pony's head away from you rather than pulling the pony around you.

Tying up

Tie the lead rope to a piece of string, which will break easily if the pony is startled and pulls back. If the pony cannot break free, it may panic even more and hurt itself. Tie the rope with a quick release knot. You can undo this quickly in an emergency by pulling the loose end.

1 Put on the saddle pad, which goes under the saddle. Place it a little too far forward to begin with.

Putting on a saddle

The saddle should sit with the pommel just in back of the withers. The girth goes about one hand's width behind the pony's elbow. You should learn how to put on a saddle even if your pony is usually tacked up when you arrive for your lessons. It is fun to do it yourself, and the more you are able to do for a pony, the better you will get to know it.

2 Lower the saddle— with the stirrups run up—onto the pad. With your left hand on the pommel, your right hand on the cantle, center the saddle on the pad. Slide the two back, smoothing the hair underneath them.

3 If there are loops on the saddle pad, slip a billet through on both sides. This will stop the pad from slipping.

4 With the girth attached on the off side, let it hang down, and bring it under the pony's belly from the near side.

5 Use the two first billets or the first and last billets. Buckle the girth loosely until you are ready to go.

Putting on a bridle

Stand on the pony's left side to put on the bridle. If it will not take the bit, wiggle your thumb in the corner of its mouth and press gently on its gums in the gap behind its bottom back teeth.

1 Take off the halter, and refasten it around the pony's neck, so it cannot walk away from you.

2 Put the reins over its head with your right hand. Hold the bridle in your left hand while you do so.

3 Slip your right arm under the pony's jaw to hold the bridle in front of its face. Press the bit into its mouth with your left hand.

All tacked up

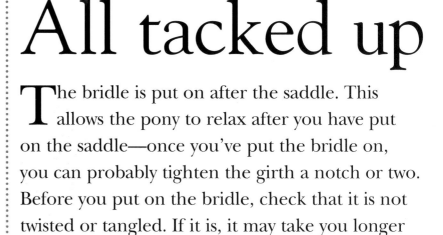

The bridle is put on after the saddle. This allows the pony to relax after you have put on the saddle—once you've put the bridle on, you can probably tighten the girth a notch or two. Before you put on the bridle, check that it is not twisted or tangled. If it is, it may take you longer to put it on, and an impatient pony may try to walk off and could get its leg caught in the reins.

Leaving a pony tacked up

If you need to leave your pony tacked up, twist the reins around each other, and fasten the throatlash through them. This stops them from going over the pony's head. Put a halter on over the bridle and tie the pony up. Loosen the girth. Do not leave your tacked-up pony unattended for long!

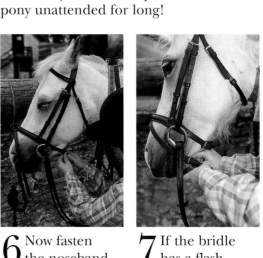

4 Fold down the pony's ears and pass the crownpiece over them. Pull out the forelock over the browband.

5 Fasten the throatlash. You should be able to fit your fist between it and the pony when it is fastened.

6 Now fasten the noseband. Make sure that you can fit two fingers underneath it when it is buckled.

7 If the bridle has a flash noseband, fasten this last. Buckle it around the pony's nose, below the bit.

Ready to go

Before mounting, always make a habit of checking the tack. Check that the bridle is on correctly, that all the straps are fastened, and that the ends have been put through their keepers. Check that the girth is not twisted and that it is fastened properly. Last of all, make sure that the girth is tight enough.

Taking tack off

Tie up your pony before removing the tack. Put the halter around its neck while you take off the bridle. Do not leave the saddle on with the girth undone—it could fall off and get damaged.

To remove the saddle, run the stirrups up the leathers. Undo the girth, and put it over the saddle. Lift off the saddle and pad together.

Carrying the bridle over your shoulder —with the noseband facing out— prevents the reins from tangling and dragging on the ground.

Carry a saddle on your forearm, with the pommel at your elbow and the girth over the seat. Carry the bridle over the same shoulder. This leaves you with one hand free to open a door or turn on a light when necessary.

To remove the bridle, undo the throatlash and noseband. Slip the bridle over the head.

Mounting and dismounting

Before you can learn to ride, you have to know how to get on and off a pony safely. Even if you use a mounting block or get a leg up, there may be times when you have to dismount and mount on your own. Check that the stirrup leathers are roughly the right length for you before mounting. Put the tips of your fingers on the stirrup bar and stretch out the leather and stirrup along your arm. The stirrup should just reach into your armpit. If not, use the buckles to adjust the length.

Getting a leg up

This is an easy way to mount. Hold the reins in your left hand and put your right hand on the saddle. Bend your left knee so your helper can hold your leg. On the count of three, spring off the ground, and your helper will lift you up at the same time.

1 Hold the reins in your left hand and carefully put your left foot in the stirrup.

2 Place your left hand on the withers, and your right hand on the cantle, and spring up off the ground.

3 Swing your right leg over the pony's hindquarters, being careful not to kick it.

4 Lower yourself gently into the saddle, and put your right foot in the stirrup.

Mounting

When you first learn to mount a pony, it is helpful if someone holds it for you. Always check that the girth is tightened before you mount, or the saddle will slide. If you do not have a helper, and your pony is inclined to wander off, stand your pony facing a gate or a wall so that it cannot move forward.

Alternative dismounting

If you are riding western, you may be taught to dismount by reversing the mounting process. Take your right foot out of the stirrup, but keep your left foot in the stirrup. Swing your right leg over the pony's hindquarters and step down, landing on the right foot first. Finally, take your left foot out of the stirrup.

Dismounting

Take both feet out of the stirrups. With the reins in your left hand, lean forward and place your hand on the withers. Put your right hand on the saddle and swing your right leg over the pony's back. Slip to the ground, bending your knees as you land. Loosen the girth before leading your pony back to the barn.

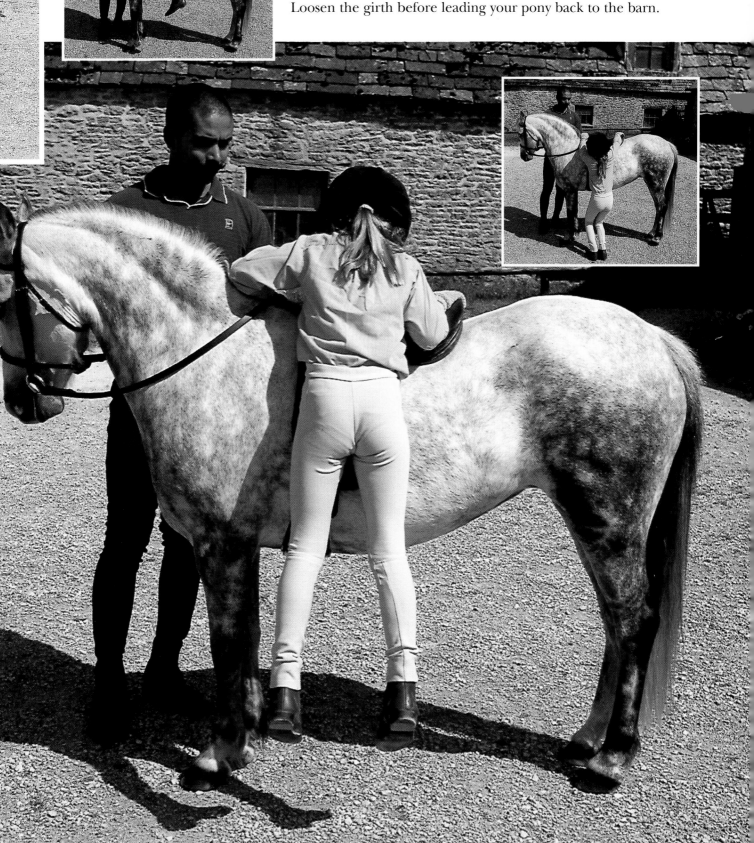

Sitting correctly

Sitting correctly in the saddle puts you in the best position to give your pony signals, called aids, to tell it what to do. The way you sit in the saddle is called your seat, and it helps you to control your pony. You need to stay supple and relaxed so that your whole body goes with the movement of your pony. Riding will then be comfortable for both of you.

Stirrup length

You can check if your stirrups are the right length by sitting in the saddle with your legs hanging down. If the tread of the stirrup is level with your ankle, the stirrups are about right.

Adjusting your stirrups

Hold the reins in one hand and adjust the stirrup with the other. Pull up the end of the leather, keeping your foot in the stirrup. When the prong is in the hole, pull down the underneath part of the leather, so the buckle is at the top.

Holding the reins

Single reins go between your little and ring fingers, and up through your hands. Hold the reins with your thumbs up. You should be able to feel a slight tension from your pony's mouth all the time. This is called the "contact." As you ride, allow your hands to move with the pony's head.

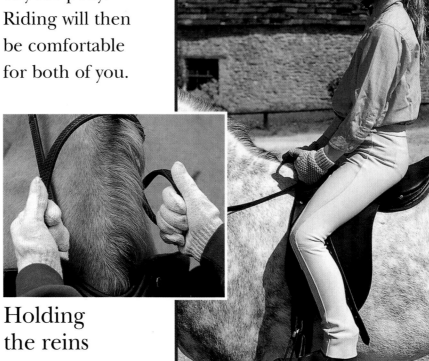

Straight line
When you are sitting in the saddle, try to imagine a line drawn straight down your body through your ear, shoulder, hip, and heel.

The correct seat

Keep your heels down and your toes pointing forward, with the balls of your feet resting on the stirrups. Your lower legs should be behind the girth, and your back should be straight. Hold your arms by your sides, with your forearms in line with the reins leading to your pony's mouth.

Sit up straight

Let your seatbones, thighs, and knees lie relaxed against the saddle

Look up and ahead of you

Relax your shoulders and elbows to allow your hands to move with the pony's head

Do not bend your wrists, but keep them relaxed

Rest your lower legs against the pony's sides

Keep your heels down

In balance
Sit square in the lowest part of the saddle. This means your weight is balanced equally on each side.

Checking the girth

To test whether the girth is tight enough, lean forward, and push two fingers under it. If there is just room for your fingers, it is all right. If there is room for more fingers, the girth needs tightening.

Keep hold of the reins with your right hand

To tighten the girth, move your leg forward, and lift the saddle flap. Pull up on the billet, and guide the buckle's prong into a higher hole with your finger.

Walking

Halt to walk

Sit up straight and "feel" the pony's mouth by gently tightening the reins. Move your weight forward, and squeeze its sides with your calves. When the pony obeys, relax the reins, but stay in contact with its mouth.

The walk is a horse or pony's slowest gait. It has four beats, with each hoof hitting the ground separately. The sequence is right hind hoof, right front hoof, left hind hoof, left front hoof, but there are always two hooves on the ground. As a horse walks, it nods its head slightly—your hands should follow this movement. Walking allows you time to concentrate on your seat and to apply the aids correctly.

Standing still
The aim when halting is to get your pony to stand square—in a balanced position. It should be ready to go forward again when you ask.

Walk to halt

Sit down deep in the saddle, and lean your weight backward slightly. Hold back on the reins, but do not pull roughly. As soon as the pony stops, relax the reins.

The walk

A pony should take even, regular steps and walk forward energetically. Its hind hooves may leave prints on the ground in front of those left by its front hooves. This is called overtracking.

Natural aids

Your lower legs are used to push your horse forward, creating the energy it needs for each movement.

Your hands control the energy created and guide the movements.

Your seat also pushes the pony forward; shifting your weight gives instructions.

Your voice can encourage your pony, slow it down, or correct it if it does not do what you want.

Turning left using a leading rein

Inside leg lies near the girth.

Outside leg is slightly behind the girth.

Western style

To ride western, sit up—do not lean like the boy in the picture—with your legs almost straight and the reins in one hand. Turn by pressing the reins against your pony's neck on the opposite side to where you want to go.

Turning left or right

To turn left, shift your weight to the left, gently pull back the left rein to increase tension (called the direct rein). Keep the right rein as it was. Place your left leg close to the girth, and your right leg behind the girth. If your horse does not respond, pull the left rein out sideways (called a leading rein) to the left. Reverse the aids to turn right.

Right turn using a leading rein

Learning to post

The trot will feel bumpy when you are riding. To even out the bumps, you can rise to the trot, or post. You lift yourself out of the saddle on one beat and sit in the saddle on the other. You can practice this while walking.

Trotting
As your pony goes into a trot, allow your hands to go with the movement of its head.

Back to walk
When you want to walk, sit down in the saddle and tighten the reins slightly.

Transitions

When you want to ask your pony to trot, shorten your reins, push the pony on slightly with your legs and seat, then relax the reins a little, allowing it to go forward. To ask your pony to slow to a walk, sit deeply in the saddle, keep your legs on its sides, and squeeze your fingers around both reins.

Posting trot

Posting means riding up and down in the saddle as a horse trots. Try not to bump around—let the horse's motion push you out of the saddle.

Asking for a trot

The trot is a two-beat gait because there are two beats to every stride. The pony's hooves hit the ground in diagonal pairs—right front hoof and left hind hoof together, then left front hoof and right hind hoof together. Trotting is faster than walking. A change of gait is called a transition. Changing to a faster gait—walk to trot—is an upward transition. Changing to a slower gait—trot to walk—is a downward transition.

Sitting trot

Your instructor will sometimes tell you to do a sitting trot. Your seatbones should stay in contact with the saddle all the time, not bump up and down. Shift your weight onto both of your seatbones and lean back a bit, your body relaxed, legs and feet in the normal position.

Diagonals

When you post, you rise as one pair of diagonal legs moves forward. In a ring, you rise as the outside foreleg goes forward. When it goes back, you sit back down in the saddle. If you are on the correct diagonal, it is easier for the pony to stay balanced. If you are on the wrong diagonal, sit in the saddle for an extra beat, then rise again. If you are on a trail ride and there is no inside or outside leg, you should change your diagonal once in a while, so your horse won't get used to one diagonal.

Lessons in cantering

A canter is a three-beat gait—the left hind hoof hits the ground, then the left front and right hind hooves together, then the right front hoof. When its legs are used in this order, a pony is on the right lead, which means its right front leg reaches farther forward than the left one. When the left front leg reaches farther forward, it is on the left lead.

Cantering

A pony can lead with either leg. If you are cantering around a ring, you should ask your pony to lead with the inside leg. It will find it easier to canter around the corners. If it leads with the outside leg, this is usually described as being on the wrong lead.

Trot to canter
Start from a sitting trot before asking your pony to canter. Stay relaxed as your pony strikes off.

Canter to trot
When your pony begins to trot, try not to let it go too fast in the first few strides.

Transitions

To canter on the right lead, put your left leg behind the girth and your right leg on the girth. Squeeze the pony's side with your left leg. Tighten the right rein. To return to a trot, sit deeply in the saddle, move both legs to the girth, and stop squeezing. Squeeze on the reins until the pony slows down.

1 Do not look down to see which lead you are on. Instead, learn to feel which of your pony's shoulders is slightly in front of the other.

2 Sit down to the canter, keeping your seatbones in contact with the saddle all the time. Sit up straight, relaxing your lower back so that your body absorbs the pony's movement.

3 When sitting to a canter on the right lead, your left shoulder and left hip should be slightly in front of your right shoulder and hip.

Cross cantering

When a pony leads with one front leg and the opposite hind leg, it is cross cantering. This can happen if it is unbalanced when it changes direction. Cross cantering is uncomfortable for both pony and rider.

Perfect canter

The canter should be a smooth, comfortable gait to sit to. Keep your pony balanced so that it takes even strides and canters in a good rhythm. If it becomes unbalanced, you should adjust its speed and energy by gently using your outside rein, inside leg, and seat.

Group lessons

Group lessons are a good way to learn to control your pony when it is with other ponies. Always leave a pony's length between your pony and the one in front. If you get too close, your pony may be kicked.

Group instructions

If you are riding at the front of the group, you are "leading the file." Your instructor may tell you to trot to the back of the ride. If everyone is to trot, the instructor will say, "Whole ride trot."

Lessons

When you have a riding lesson, it could be in an indoor or an outdoor ring, private lessons, or with a group. You can learn a lot during lessons, not only from what you do yourself, but from what you see other riders doing. As you learn how to control your pony during lessons, you will gradually gain confidence.

Changing the rein

In a lesson, you will ride in both directions around the ring. When you change direction, it is called changing the rein. You can do this in several ways, such as by riding across the diagonal.

In the ring

Points in a ring and a dressage arena are marked with a letter. International-sized arenas have extra letters. You need to learn the standard letters, because your instructor will give you specific movements to do in the ring.

To remember the standard letters, use a phrase, like "All King Edward's Horses Can Make Big Fences."

Arena diagram:
C H M E B 40m K F A 20m

A figure eight is made up of two equal circles. Riding a figure eight requires two changes of rein.

The diagonal goes between two corners—for example, F to H. F to E is known as a short diagonal.

Serpentine loops go from one side of the ring to the other. All the loops must be the same size.

A 5m loop is a curve of a maximum of 5m in from the long side of the ring toward the center.

Circles can be ridden at several points in the ring. You may be asked to ride a 10m, 15m, or 20m circle.

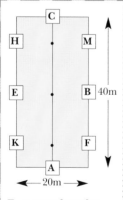

Practice on your own

There is a lot to think about when you are having a lesson. You must listen to the instructor and concentrate on controlling your pony. If you can, practice what you have been taught between lessons.

Private lessons

These are the best lessons to have when you are first learning to ride. The instructor can give you all of his attention, and you can concentrate fully on the particular thing you are trying to learn.

Group lessons

If your instructor asks all the riders in your lesson to carry out different exercises at the same time, you may have to ride past another pony. Ride "left hand to left hand" past a pony going in the opposite direction.

Lessons on the lunge

Having a lesson on a lunge line is a good way to improve your seat. The instructor uses a lunge rein and a long whip to control the pony for you, leaving you free to concentrate on your riding position.

No reins

Although you may feel insecure at first, riding without reins teaches you how to balance in the saddle. This means you will be less likely to pull on the reins and hurt your pony's mouth when things go wrong.

No stirrups

Riding without stirrups is a good way of learning how to sit while trotting. Cross the stirrups over the pony's withers so that they do not hit its sides. Sit deep in the saddle and stretch your legs down.

Exercises in the saddle

Doing exercises during lessons on your pony is fun, and they will help keep you supple. When you have done the exercises a few times, you will be much more confident with your riding skills. To begin with, do not do any exercises on your own. Wait until an instructor is present to hold the pony.

Lungeing cavesson

Lungeing is a good way to exercise a pony when you cannot ride it or if you want to use up some of its energy before doing so. Ask it to walk, trot, and canter in both directions.

For lungeing a pony wears a special halter called a lungeing cavesson. The lunge rein is attached to a swivel ring on the front. The swivel prevents the rein from tangling as the pony circles around you.

Pony in a lungeing cavesson

Stretching up
Hold your arms above your head and stretch up as high as you can.

Stretching forward
Lean forward along your pony's neck. Keep your head to one side.

Stretching exercises

There are many different stretching exercises you can do. The best time to do them is before a lesson, to warm up your muscles. You can stretch up and forward, backward to lie on the pony's rump, or down to touch your opposite toe.

Around the world

This is always fun to do. First, swing your right leg over the pony's neck, so you are facing the side. Then, swing your left leg over its rump, so you are facing its tail. Next, swing your right leg over its rump, so you are facing the opposite side. Finally, swing your left leg over its neck, so you are sitting facing the front again.

Ankle stretch

With your stirrups crossed over the saddle and your legs hanging down loosely, point your toes down toward the ground as far as you can, then point them up. Point them to the right and to the left, without turning your legs.

Going for a trail ride

Once you have learned to ride, it is fun to go out for a trail ride with friends. You will have to cope with all kinds of situations, and you may find your pony behaves differently. If you are still a beginner, you must be accompanied by a responsible adult or your instructor. Even if you are an experienced rider, always tell someone where you are going and what time you expect to return.

Lead line

When you ride on your first trail ride, you may go on a lead line in case you cannot manage your pony out in the open. An experienced rider will hold a long rein attached to your pony's bit. She will have overall control of your pony.

Opening a gate

If the catch on a gate is easy to operate, you can open it without dismounting. Ride your pony right up to the gate so that you can reach out and operate the catch. Push the gate open and, if possible, hold on to it while you walk through. Make sure it doesn't swing back and hit your pony. Once through, you have to close the gate.

Trail ride manners

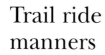

If a trail goes along the edge of a field, you must stay on it. You may be able to have a canter if there are no animals in the field.

Through water

If you have to cross a stream or a flooded field, let your pony take its time. Ponies are reluctant to go through water until they know there is a firm base on which to walk.

Coming home

You can enjoy cantering and trotting on your ride, but always walk for the last ten minutes on the way home to let your pony cool down. Never bring a pony back to its stable hot and sweating, because it could catch a chill.

After the ride

When you get home on a hot day, sponge down your pony where it has sweated under the saddle, then walk it around until it is dry. Otherwise, brush the saddle patch, brush off any mud, and check its legs for thorns and scratches.

Reflective safety wear

Do not ride on the road at night. If you have to ride when the light is poor, wear clothes that reflect car headlights. You can get a reflective hat cover and vest for yourself, and an exercise sheet, tail guard, bridle cover, and leg bands for your pony. You can even get lights to attach to your stirrups.

Asking drivers to slow down
If your pony or the one behind you is nervous of traffic, do not be afraid to ask a driver to slow down, especially if it is a large or noisy vehicle. Hold your outside arm out to the side and move it up and down slowly in a wide arc.

Riding on the road

Never ride on your own on the road unless you are sure you can control your pony in any situation. Avoid narrow roads without grass shoulders, and keep off main roads if you can. Learn to use the correct hand signals, and study the rules of the road—they apply to you as well as drivers. Be polite to road users and thank drivers who slow down or stop for you— they are then more likely to do it for other riders.

Hand signals

Make signals clearly and in plenty of time. Hold your reins firmly in the other hand so that you keep control of your pony. When you are riding in a group, keep together so that you do not hold up traffic unnecessarily. The rider at the front and back of a single file should make the hand signals. If you are riding in pairs, the riders on the inside of the turn should signal.

Turning right
To tell drivers that you want to turn right, hold your right arm out straight. Check that it is safe before you turn.

Stop
To ask traffic to stop, hold up your right hand high in front of you.

Turning left
To tell drivers that you want to turn left, hold out your left arm. Keep it straight so that your intentions are clear.

Thank you
To say "thank you" to a driver, raise your hand and smile. If you need to keep both hands on the reins, nod your head clearly so that the driver sees.

On the bit

When the pony is balanced between your hands and legs and you have soft contact with the bit, it is "on the bit." It will hold its head straight, with its mouth lower than your hands. This position allows maximum control and feeling of your pony's motion.

Simple dressage

Once you have learned to control your pony and you are confident doing basic gaits in the ring, you may progress to more advanced riding and simple dressage movements, called training on the flat. Even if you do not go on to enter any competitions, careful training will help you learn to communicate with your pony and get the most from it.

Square halt

With practice you will be able to do a square halt where the front and back hooves are perfectly in line with each other. Your weight must be distributed evenly so your pony stays balanced.

Turning on the forehand

The horse's hindlegs move around its inside foreleg. To turn to the right, tighten the right rein, bring the left rein over in support, press with your left leg, and hold the hindquarters steady with your right leg.

Shoulder-in
The horse's front legs follow an inner track. It crosses its front legs as it travels, but its hind legs move straight forward.

Lateral work

Lateral means "sideways." In lateral work, the horse's body forms a curve, so its front legs move on a different track from its hind legs. For this reason, lateral work is also known as "work on two tracks."

Travers
The horse's hind legs follow an inner track. Its body is bent to the outside of the ring.

Leg yield
The horse moves forward and sideways away from the rider's leg. Its body is straight.

R

Riding sidesaddle

To ride sidesaddle, you face front, with your right leg over a pommel called the fixed head. Your left leg rests under another pommel—the leaping head. It is supported by a single stirrup. The saddle is secured by a girth and a balance strap. A pony has special training to carry a sidesaddle and responds to a whip on the right side instead of the rider's leg.

Counter canter

Horses and ponies normally lead with their inside leg when they canter, but for a movement called the counter canter, they need to lead with their outside leg. This is difficult to perform, and the horse needs to be well balanced.

Advanced riding

If you watch a top-class dressage partnership, the horse seems to carry out perfect movements effortlessly, and the rider gives no visible aids. However, it will take lots of practice before you will be able to carry out such advanced dressage gaits and movements properly. Even the best riders were not born champions. They have spent many years working hard and patiently.

The art of riding

The classical art of riding is practiced by the Spanish Riding School of Vienna in Austria and the Cadre Noir of Saumur in France. Riders at these schools perform complicated steps based on the horse's natural movements. This horse is performing a levade—a controlled half rear.

Spanish School

Turn on the haunches

This is when a horse pivots around its inside hind leg, which should remain still. It uses its other legs in the same sequence as it does when going forward.

Collection and extension

To "collect" a horse is to shorten its frame, making it push off its haunches. Its stride is shorter and more bouncy, and the gait is slower. Extension is the opposite. The horse stretches out its head and neck, and it takes longer, lower strides, increasing its speed.

Collected to extended walk
As the horse moves from a collected walk, through a medium walk, into an extended walk, it gradually lengthens its stride and stretches out its head and neck.

Collected walk

Collected trot
The horse moves at a steady, collected gait, but still with energy. Its head and neck are raised and its hindquarters appear lower.

Extended trot
The horse is moving much faster, with a longer stride. As it extends the trot, it flicks its front hooves forward.

Flying change

When a horse changes its lead while cantering, when all its feet are off the ground, it is called a "flying change." It is a difficult movement to perform. An experienced horse and rider may do a flying change every stride.

Half-pass

This is a lateral movement in which the horse moves forward and sideways at the same time. It crosses its outside legs over, in front of the inside legs, bending its head in the direction in which it is going. This horse (right) is moving to the left.

In the air
This horse has changed lead in the air and is now on a right lead.

Collected/medium walk

Medium walk

Extended walk

Free walk on a long rein

Collected canter
The collected canter is a slow, rocking gait. The horse must be supple and relaxed. The rider should sit deep in the saddle and follow the movement.

Extended canter
The horse stretches its neck and lengthens its stride to cover as much ground as possible. Its weight, and that of the rider, move forward.

Riding at top speed

Galloping is very exciting for both pony and rider. Do not attempt it until you are sure you can control your pony at a canter. Choose a good place to gallop. A smooth field with an uphill slope is ideal—it is easier to stop when going uphill! Never gallop over rough ground, near or up to other ponies, or in a confined space. Make sure there is plenty of room to maneuver.

Half seat position

When you gallop, you should go into a half seat position, or galloping position. This means leaning forward and placing your weight on your knees and feet. Raise your rear just clear of the saddle, but keep your balance. Practice the position while stationary.

Asking for a gallop

Get your pony into a good canter, and get into a half seat position. Urge your pony forward with your legs until you are going fast enough for the canter to become a gallop. Keep contact with its mouth through the reins.

The gallop

The gallop is the fastest gait. It is a four-beat gait, with each hoof hitting the ground separately. When the left front leg is leading, the sequence is right hind, left hind, right front, and then left front.

Body position
When you are in a half seat position, keep your head up, and look where you are going.

Suspension
There is a moment in a gallop when all four hooves are off the ground.

Slowing down

Ponies love to gallop, and they can be difficult to stop. When you want to slow down to a canter, maintain contact with your legs and sit back in the saddle, taking an upright position again. Resist the forward movement with the reins until the pony slows down.

Fast forward

The average pony gallops at around 15 mph (24km/h). This may not sound fast, but when you are thundering along with the wind whistling past your ears, it feels it! The Thoroughbred is the fastest horse in the world. It gallops about 30 mph (50km/h), but its record race speed is an amazing 43 mph (69.2km/h) over a quarter of a mile.

Trotting over poles

When you walk or trot over poles on the ground, it teaches you and your pony to develop balance and rhythm. It shows you both how to approach an obstacle with confidence and helps you to judge distances.

Keep your head up and look ahead.

Let the pony stretch its neck forward.

Your pony should take even strides

. . . and tuck its legs up over the poles.

First lessons in jumping

Once you have learned to ride and you have a good, secure seat in the saddle, you can start learning how to jump, called "training over fences." There are five stages to a jump—approach, takeoff, suspension in the air, landing, and recovery. As a pony jumps, it stretches its head and neck forward. Stretch with it in a jumping position.

Between the wings

For practice, first trot between the wings of a jump in a jumping position—shorten your stirrups and lean forward over the pony's neck, pushing your arms forward so your elbows are slightly in front of your body. Next, ride through with a pole on the ground.

Jumping tips

Always push your pony forward with confidence; do not hesitate. If you are unsure, your pony will be worried.

Plan your approach carefully so that you meet the fence straight on.

Do not panic if things go wrong. Ask yourself what it was you did wrong, and try to do better next time.

A refusal

First jump

Approaching the jump, shorten the reins, but do not restrain the pony. On takeoff, get in jumping position, and do not look down. Gently return to the saddle as you land, keeping your heels down. If you need to, hold on to the mane to prevent jerking the pony's mouth.

Getting larger

Once you are confident jumping a low rail, you can try something more ambitious. A good way to progress is to keep the fences low, but make them wider. A wide fence, called a spread, makes your pony stretch out further to clear it.

Top-class jumping

To clear huge fences like this, the horse has to stretch its head and neck right out.

Jumping higher

If you want to do really well at show jumping, you need to spend a lot of time practicing with your pony. You will need to train on the flat as well as practice over fences. Flat work is important because your pony needs to be supple and obedient to jump well. It must listen to your commands so it does not rush the fences or take off at the wrong moment. When you are jumping, whether for practice or in the ring, you should push your pony with your seat and legs so it knows for certain what you want it to do.

Seeing a distance

Three or four strides before a fence, try to judge how many strides your pony needs before takeoff. This is called "seeing a distance." If a pony is too near a fence, it will not be able to jump. Too far away, it may knock down a pole.

Water jump

A water jump is a wide pool of water with a low fence on the takeoff side. The horse has to stretch out to jump over the obstacle without putting a foot in it.

Double combination

Four fence combination

Combination

Two or more fences close together count as one obstacle, called a combination. If a horse refuses at one part, it has to jump the whole sequence again. The number of strides between fences in a combination can vary.

Owning your own pony

O wning a pony is a lot of fun, but also a huge responsibility. You must learn how to care for it properly. If it is stabled in your own barn, you will need to put in hours of hard work every day. If it lives in a pasture, you must tend to it in all kinds of weather. Even if your pony is boarded, you will still spend a lot of time looking after it.

Put your pony first
No matter how tired or hungry you are when you come back from a ride, you must always see to the pony's needs first.

Heavy chores
Much of the work of looking after a pony involves lifting heavy objects like buckets of water and bales of hay. Learn how to lift things correctly, so you do not injure yourself.

Pasture kept

Many ponies live out in a pasture all the time, and others only part of the time. It is more natural for them than living in a stable, and less work for you. But they cannot live in just any pasture. It must be fenced and free of hazards, such as barbed wire, and it must have a water supply. You should clear it of poisonous plants, and there should be shade from the sun and shelter from the wind and rain.

Pasture care

Pastures grazed by horses and ponies need to be taken care of. They need to be mowed, harrowed, and rolled in the spring to level the ground. Ideally, they should also be grazed by cattle or sheep, which eat the grass horses will not touch.

Water and fencing

Post and rail is the ideal fencing for horses, but it is expensive. Sagging barbed-wire fences are especially dangerous and can cause horrific injuries. A self-filling water trough saves a lot of work, but must be cleaned out regularly to get rid of algae.

Living outside

In the wild, horses and ponies can travel to find food. In a pasture, they can eat only what is there. If there are too many ponies in a pasture, they will not get enough to eat. There should be about one horse or two ponies per acre of good grazing pasture.

A run-in shelter

A three-sided shelter protects a pony from the wind and stormy weather. The pony may also use it in hot weather to get away from flies. A mineral lick can supply nutrients not found in the grass.

Picking up droppings

It is important to clean the droppings out of the pasture regularly, especially if it is not very large and is grazed by a lot of ponies. Not only do piles of droppings kill the grass, but if they are left lying around, they encourage parasitic worms to breed.

Poisonous plants

Many plants are poisonous if eaten in large quantities; a few are deadly even in small amounts. One of the most dangerous plants that you are likely to find in fields is tansy. It is tall, with ragged leaves and small, yellow, daisylike flowers. It is very dangerous, whether fresh or dried, and you should pull it up and destroy it. Sprinkle salt on the remains of its roots in the ground to kill them, too.

Rhododendron can be deadly to animals

Tansy should be pulled up and burned

Yew is deadly, even in small amounts

Foxglove can be deadly, but is not often eaten

Buttercups are mildly poisonous, but safe in hay

Acorns in large amounts are poisonous

Hemlock contains a deadly poison

Henbane is very poisonous, and ponies like it

Horsetail is poisonous fresh or dried in hay

Laburnum is highly poisonous

Laurel contains cyanide and can be deadly

Pasture-kept pony care

1 Approach a pony from the front and walk toward its shoulder, holding out a treat in your hand so it can see it.

2 While it eats the treat, slip the lead rope around its neck in case it tries to move away from you.

3 Put the halter over its nose, and bring the crown-piece around to buckle it on the near side.

4 With your right hand under the pony's jaw and your left hand at the end of the lead rope, lead the pony in.

You need to visit a pasture-kept pony every day. Even if you are not going to ride or feed it, you should check that it is all right at least once, and preferably twice a day. In the winter you must check its blanket if it wears one. You may need to take it off and put it on again to make the pony comfortable. Walk around the pasture to check the fencing. Make sure the gate is shut and that there is nothing dangerous on the ground.

Breaking the ice

In cold weather, you may find that you need to break the ice on the water trough several times a day. Leaving a large rubber ball in the trough to float around helps prevent the water from freezing over.

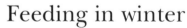

Catching a pony

Some ponies are easier to catch than others. If yours is difficult, visit it with a treat, whether you are going to catch it or not. Never chase it around the pasture. Wait for it to come to you.

Feeding in winter

In the winter, there is not as much grass available to eat. Ponies living outside will need hay and possibly some grain and pellets to supplement the grass. The amount depends on how much work they do, their age, and their condition.

Turning a pony out

To put a pony in its pasture, or turn it out, lead it through the gate and close it. Take the pony into the field, and turn it to face the gate before quietly removing its halter, giving it a pat, and walking away. Do not wave your arms to make it gallop off.

Having fun

Ponies do not mind the cold, and it can make them very lively. But they do not like rain and wind. A clipped pony must wear a waterproof blanket to keep it warm and dry. Most outdoor blankets have secure fastenings and allow ponies to move freely.

Good barn management

Toys

Horses and ponies kept in stalls for long periods can get bored. You can buy special toys, like a ball hung by string, to entertain them. Attach a treat or salt lick to the string, or smear the ball with molasses.

If you decide to keep your pony in a barn, you need to make sure the space is suitable for it. A 10- x 10-foot stall is large enough for most ponies, but horses require more space. Specifically designed barns made of brick, wood, or concrete blocks are best, but all kinds of buildings can be turned into a barn. The stall door should be in two parts, so that the top part can be left open. Horses and ponies like to look out over the door and watch what is going on around them. A busy stable keeps them entertained when they are in their stalls.

Barn routine

You will need to visit a stabled pony several times a day. It has to be fed, given hay and water, and its stall must be mucked out—even if you are not going to ride it. It should also be turned out, so it can exercise. All these things take time and have to fit around other commitments, like school, homework, and family. If your pony is boarded, some of these chores may be done by the staff at the barn, but you should try to take part in your pony's care as much as possible.

Find someone to help you look after and exercise your pony. Sharing a pony can work well if you have an agreement as to who is going to do what. You can share the expenses, too.

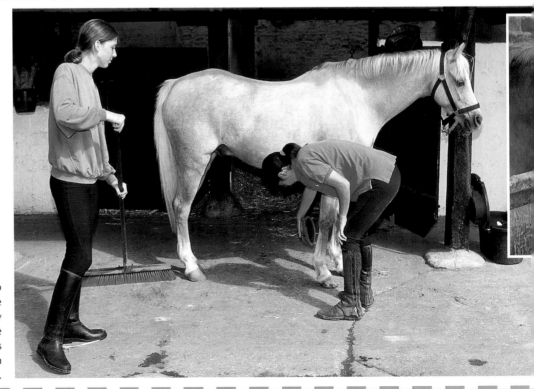

American barn
A large barn with box stalls on both sides of a wide, central aisle and doors at both ends of the barn is called an "American barn."

The ideal stable

The ideal stable is light and well ventilated. It must be waterproof and draft-free, but with good air circulation. It is best situated where the pony can see people and other animals coming and going.

Fixtures and fittings

There are lots of things you can have in a barn to make life easier for you and your pony. You may consider having a hayrack and an automatic watering system. Crossties, which are attached to each side of the aisle and clip onto the halter, are convenient for holding your pony while you groom it.

Box stall
A horse must have plenty of room to lie down. The floor of the stall must be nonslip.

Ventilation
Windows must be protected by heavy wire mesh. They should open in a way that allows air in, but keeps rain out.

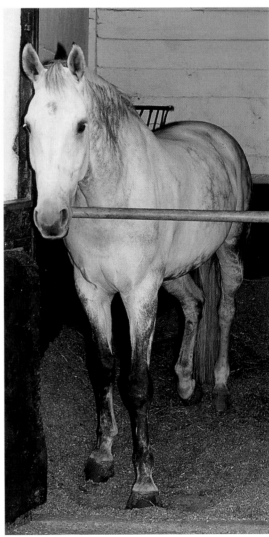

Door hook
Use a hook on the wall to hold the top of the stable door open.

Safety light
A light should be covered and placed high up—out of your pony's reach.

Stable bolt
This locks on the outside so that your pony cannot open the door.

Horses and ponies have efficient built-in clocks and know very well when their next meal is due. Work out a timetable for feeding, and try to stick to it at all times—weekends and holidays included.

Kick bolt
This is placed at the bottom of the door. You operate it with your foot, which is useful if your hands are full.

Door bar
When you can keep an eye on your pony, a bar, a chain with a rubber coating, or a webbing net across the door frame should be enough to keep it in.

Mucking out

You must keep your pony's stall clean. This means removing the droppings—"skipping out"—and cleaning the stall thoroughly—"mucking out"—every day. If your pony comes in for just a short time in the day, you can leave the floor bare after mucking out, but you must put down the bedding if it is in at night. Some people use a "deep-litter system" to save time and bedding. They leave the wet bedding for a week or more and take out only the droppings.

How to muck out

When you muck out a stall thoroughly, you remove all the wet bedding from underneath, as well as the droppings. It is best to do this when the pony is out of the stall. You can leave the floor to dry for a while before putting down new bedding.

Mucking out equipment

The basic things you need to muck out a stable are a large muck bucket for collecting droppings, a broom, a shovel, a pitchfork, and a wheelbarrow. Different pitchforks are made for different bedding. You can use a four-pronged pitchfork for straw or one with many prongs for wood shavings.

1 First pick up any droppings you can see. Then, using a pitchfork, pile all the clean straw against the walls. You will reuse it later.

2 Use a pitchfork to pick up the wet straw and any droppings mixed in with it. Put the wet straw in a wheelbarrow to take to the manure pile.

3 Sweep the floor with a stiff broom to clean up any remaining dirt and bits of straw. Shovel these into the wheelbarrow too.

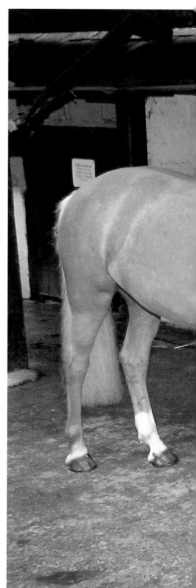

Straw
Straw is comfortable, but ponies often eat it. Some ponies are allergic to the fungal spores in straw, and it makes them cough.

Rubber
This can be used for ponies with a dust allergy, but it is not very comfortable. A thin layer of shavings can be put on top.

Wood shavings
These are more expensive than straw, but they are good for ponies who are allergic to straw. They take time to rot down.

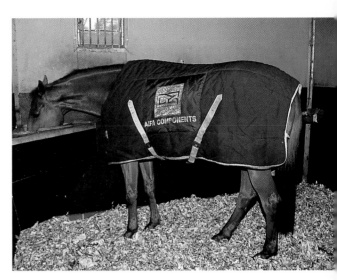

Shredded paper
This is made from old newspapers and provides a warm, dust-free bed. It is cheap, but it becomes soggy and difficult to handle when it is wet.

Types of bedding

A pony needs bedding in its stall so that it can lie down and rest. The bedding also stops it from jarring its feet on the hard floor. There are several different types of bedding. You should choose the one that suits your pony.

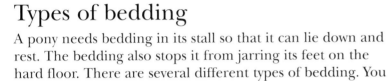

4 Empty the wheelbarrow at the manure pile. Keep the manure pile stacked neatly to decompose better.

5 Put back the clean straw, and add new straw on top. Leave banks of straw around the walls.

Feeding a healthy diet

Ponies naturally feed on grass—their instinct is to eat constantly, a small amount at a time. They need to eat a lot to get enough nourishment. If your pony is stabled, or in steady work, it may need hay and a concentrated feed for extra energy. Be careful—a pony will eat until it is sick if you give it an unlimited supply.

Dried sugar beet must be soaked before feeding

Bran is high in fiber

Sweet feed is well balanced

Packaged grass is dust free

Soaked sugar beet is ready to eat

Micronized barley is easily digested

Pellets are easy to feed

Chaff (chopped straw) is mixed with other feed

Roots and fruits

Ponies love apples and root vegetables such as carrots. These are a great treat, but they must be cut up in the right way so that your pony does not choke. Apples should be cut into slices, and carrots should be sliced lengthwise.

Different feeds

You can mix your own ingredients to make a balanced diet, but sweet feed and pellets are easiest because they are complete, balanced feeds in themselves. Never feed your pony grass cuttings, because they are likely to give it severe stomach pains called colic.

Feeding treats

All ponies enjoy treats such as apples, carrots, mints, and the treats you can buy at tack shops and feed stores. Try to give treats only as a reward for being good. If you give too many treats, some ponies will expect them all the time and may nip you as you walk past.

Rules of feeding

Feed little and often, never just one huge bucket of food. A pony has a small stomach.

Give your pony mostly bulky, fibrous food, called roughage, such as grass or hay.

Match the amount of food you give a pony with the amount of work it is doing.

Make sure your pony has clean, fresh water available at all times.

Never feed old or musty food, or hay that is moldy.

Feed your pony at regular times, and keep its buckets clean.

Never guess how much food to give a pony. Weigh it.

Do not feed your pony right before or after it has done work.

Soaking a haynet

Some ponies are allergic to the dust and fungal spores in hay. They give the ponies a kind of asthma, and they cough. This affects their performance, making fast work impossible. To remove some of the dust and spores, you can soak hay in a tub of water—a plastic garbage can works well. Allow the hay to drain before feeding it.

Hanging a haynet

A good way to feed hay is in a haynet, rather than loose on the ground. It stops your pony from trampling on the hay and wasting it. Weigh the full haynet so that you know how much you are giving. Hang the net high enough to stop your pony from getting a foot stuck in it, but not so high that hay and seeds will fall in its eyes. .

1 Before you start to fill a haynet, open the the top fully to make it easier to push the hay in. Ask a friend to help, or use a foot to keep the net open.

2 To hang up the net, pull the string through the ring on the stable wall. A haynet can be quite heavy, so support it from underneath.

3 Pass the string through the bottom of the net, then pull up the net as high as you can. Tie a quick release knot around the string to hold it.

Water brush   Sponge   Sweat scraper

Curry comb

Stable cloth

Hoof oil and brush

Hoof pick

Body brush

Mane comb (for pulling)

Dandy brush

Grooming kit

There are many different items you can have in a grooming kit, but you only need a few basic items, each designed for a specific job. Keep them in a box and use them only on one pony. A shared kit can spread skin diseases.

Grooming and washing

Y ou should groom your pony every day. It is hard work, but it will help tone your pony's muscles as well as keep its skin and coat clean. If your pony lives in a pasture, it will need less grooming. Just brush off the dried mud, comb out its mane and tail, and pick out its hooves before you ride. Excess brushing or bathing can remove oils from the coat, which keep the pony warm and waterproof.

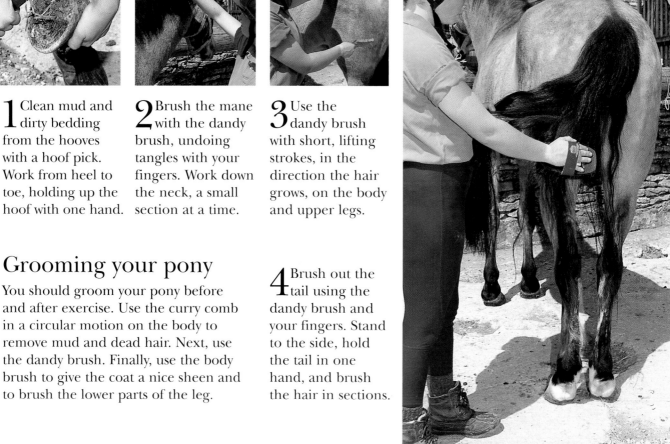

1 Clean mud and dirty bedding from the hooves with a hoof pick. Work from heel to toe, holding up the hoof with one hand.

2 Brush the mane with the dandy brush, undoing tangles with your fingers. Work down the neck, a small section at a time.

3 Use the dandy brush with short, lifting strokes, in the direction the hair grows, on the body and upper legs.

Grooming your pony

You should groom your pony before and after exercise. Use the curry comb in a circular motion on the body to remove mud and dead hair. Next, use the dandy brush. Finally, use the body brush to give the coat a nice sheen and to brush the lower parts of the leg.

4 Brush out the tail using the dandy brush and your fingers. Stand to the side, hold the tail in one hand, and brush the hair in sections.

Washing your pony

Give your pony a bath only on a warm, sunny day so it does not get a chill. If the weather is not good, but you want to clean your pony up, you can wash its mane and tail and any white socks. Take great care to keep shampoo out of its eyes, and make sure you rinse the soap out thoroughly.

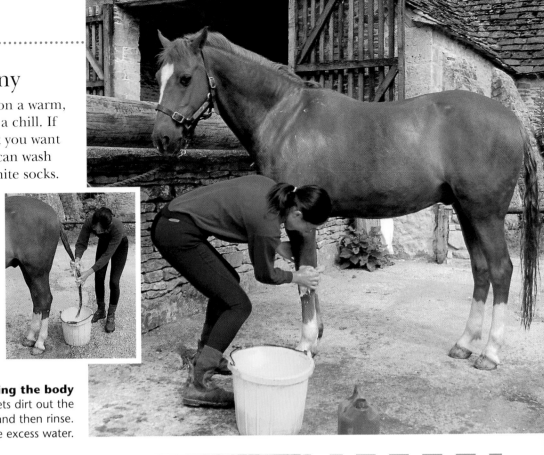

Washing the tail
Use a bucket of water to wash the tail. Lift the bucket so you get in as much tail as possible. Wet the tail, shampoo it, then rinse until it is squeaky clean.

Washing the body
Warm water from a bucket gets dirt out the best. Shampoo with a sponge and then rinse. Use a sweat scraper to remove excess water.

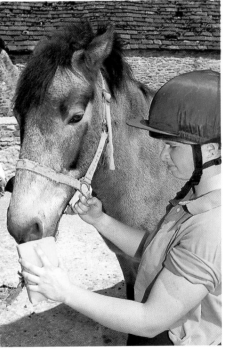

5 To brush your pony's face, take off its halter, and fasten it around its neck. Brush gently with the body brush.

6 Clean your pony's eyes and nose with a damp sponge. Use a different sponge to wash the dock area under its tail.

Grooming tips

Clean the dandy and body brush with a metal curry comb after every three strokes.

Cleaning a body brush

Finish off the mane and tail by "laying" them down in the correct position with a damp brush or comb.

Use a stable cloth to give your pony's coat a final polish. Wipe it over its body in the direction that the coat lies.

Brush on hoof oil to make the hooves shiny and clean. Put it on clean, dry hooves.

Oiling a hoof

Clipping and blankets

In the winter, horses and ponies grow long, thick coats that keep them warm. If they are worked hard and fast, they sweat a lot and can lose condition. They will take a long time to dry and might get a chill. To avoid this, working horses and ponies have their coats clipped in a variety of patterns. When clipped horses and ponies are resting, they need to wear a blanket, both in their stall and in the pasture, to compensate for their lack of warm winter coat.

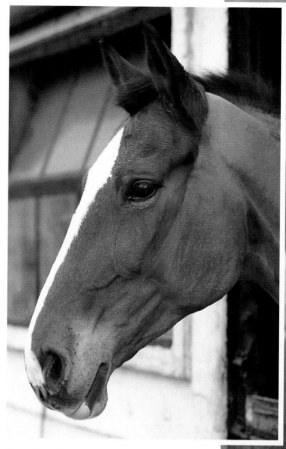

Bandit clip
The horse is clipped up to its ears, leaving the hair on the front of its face for protection against rain.

Types of clips

A horse may be fully clipped or just partly clipped. The type of clip chosen depends on the individual horse and the work it is going to do. It is important to remove hair where it is most likely to sweat.

Clipping

Your pony must be clean and dry to be clipped. The person doing the clip may mark the shape in chalk first. Once a pony is used to the noise, the clippers are worked against the lie of its coat.

Bib clip (horse not worked much) The hair on the head, front of the neck, chest, and shoulders is clipped off. The rest is left.

Blanket clip (competition horse) A "blanket" area on the quarters and back, and the legs, is left unclipped. The rest is clipped.

Chaser clip (worked 2–3 times a week) The line of clipping goes from the ear to the stifle. Steeplechasers may be clipped like this.

Hunter clip (competition horse) Just the saddle patch and legs are left unclipped to prevent soreness and to protect against thorns.

Using a stable blanket

1 Fold the blanket or sheet in half, and place it on the pony's back. Put it farther forward than it will finally fit.

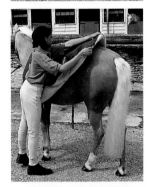

2 Unfold the back section of the blanket and pull it down over your pony's hindquarters, smoothing its coat flat as you do this.

3 Fasten the straps at the front. Check that the blanket is in the right position and not too tight on your pony's shoulders.

4 When you are satisfied the blanket is on comfortably, attach the surcingles (crossed straps) under its belly and the leg straps, if there are any.

New Zealand blanket
This heavy winter blanket is waterproof and has a warm lining.

Types of blankets

There are many different types of blankets, and each is designed for a different purpose. Some are for keeping ponies warm and dry, while others are for keeping them clean. They are made from a variety of materials.

Fly sheet
This light sheet keeps a horse clean and keeps off the flies. It is useful for traveling to summer shows.

Sweat sheet
This cotton sheet used with hot, sweating racehorses and competition horses dries them so they do not get a chill.

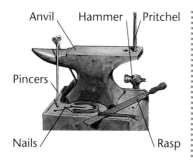

Anvil Hammer Pritchel
Pincers
Nails Rasp

A farrier's tools

Pictured are some of the tools a farrier uses. He hammers red-hot shoes into shape on an anvil and carries them on a spike called a pritchel.

Stamped plain shoe | Fullered shoe | Light racing shoe

Hole for a stud, for extra grip

Heavy shoe for draft horse

Types of shoes

Some horseshoes are made of iron; others, especially racehorse shoes, are made of aluminum. The kind of shoe a horse has depends on the work it does. Some correct hoof problems, and some have a groove, called fullering, for better grip.

Hot shoeing

Shoeing is often done hot because the shoes can then be altered easily to fit the pony's hooves. Once the shoe is on, the farrier taps the shoe gently into place, and finishes off the hoof with a rasp.

Shoes and shoeing

Horses' and ponies' hooves grow all the time—just like fingernails—and need trimming about every six weeks. If a horse is worked on a hard surface like a road, its hooves wear down quickly and get sore, so they are shod for protection. Every few weeks, a farrier, or blacksmith, removes the shoes, trims the hooves, and reshoes a horse. Shoeing does not hurt.

1 The farrier cuts the clenches, or nail ends, on the old shoe, then levers it off with pincers.

2 Then he trims the hoof with a pair of hoof cutters and cleans up the hoof with a rasp.

3 The farrier heats a new shoe in the furnace, then shapes it on the anvil.

4 He tries the hot shoe on the hoof. When it is the right fit, he cools it in water.

5 He hammers the nails through the hoof to the side, where he twists off the ends.

6 He bends the ends of the nails down to form the clenches, which hold the shoe in place.

Nailing on the shoe
The farrier hammers the nails through the shoe into the underside of the hoof, and they emerge at the side.

Protective clothing
A farrier wears a leather apron to protect his legs when he is working.

A farrier's job
It is important for your pony that its hooves are well shod, and being a farrier is a skilled job. Most farriers travel to their customers with a mobile, gas-fired forge, in which they heat the shoes. Some farriers do not have a mobile forge, and do cold shoeing—when the shoes are not heated.

Toolbox
This box contains all the farrier's tools except the anvil.

Keeping your pony healthy

A healthy pony has bright eyes, a shiny coat, and a good appetite. You should worm and vaccinate your pony regularly. But, still, there will be times when it is not well. It may seem depressed, or it may have lost its appetite. Or it may have obvious symptoms, such as lameness, a runny nose, or a cough. If you spot any of these signs of illness, you may need to call the veterinarian.

Teeth floating

A pony's back teeth can wear unevenly. It may find it hard to chew or may have a sore mouth. Ask a horse dentist or vet to check your pony's teeth twice a year. He will use a gag so he is not bitten, then file, or float, the teeth smooth.

Worming treatments

Grazing horses pick up worms easily. Worms live in a horse's intestines and take the nutrients from its food. It will lose weight and may die if it is not treated. To prevent this, it must be wormed twice a year. The treatment can be in the form of a paste squirted into its mouth or a powder mixed with its food.

Vaccinations

Every year, a pony should have vaccinations for equine infectious anemia and tetanus, because both diseases can be fatal. A vet will do this for you. It may look painful, but most ponies do not mind it. Keep your pony's vaccination records safe because you may need to produce them at shows.

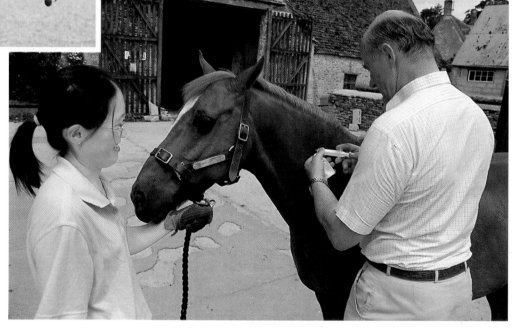

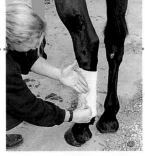

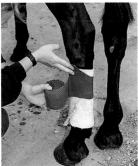

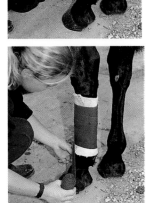

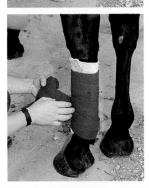

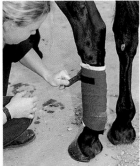

Leg wraps

First, wrap a layer of leg quilts around the pony's leg. Start the wrap, or bandage, at the top and work down the leg, overlapping each layer. Keep the leg quilts flat. Make a V-shape with the wrap at the bottom, then work back up. Try to secure the wrap on the outside of the leg. Always bandage both front legs or both hind legs, not just one.

Wound first aid

Your pony may get small cuts and scratches, especially if it spends time in a pasture. Most of the time you can treat these without calling the vet. Treat small wounds with an antiseptic spray, ointment, or powder, which helps heal the wound and also keeps flies away.

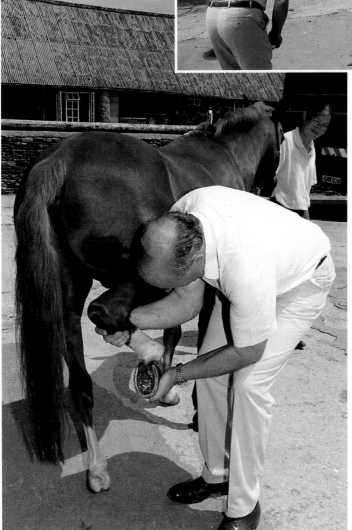

Trotting up
To check for lameness, the vet will ask you to walk and trot the pony on a level, hard surface. The vet will then be able to tell on which leg it is lame.

Calling the vet

If you cannot deal with a problem, call the vet. Never leave your pony for more than 24 hours with a problem no one can explain. Make a careful note of any symptoms, so that you can give the vet as much accurate information as possible.

Flexion test
The vet may do a flexion test to check for lameness. This involves bending up a leg tightly and holding it for a few moments before releasing it and immediately trotting the pony. Any lameness will then be obvious.

Taking part in events

You may simply enjoy pleasure riding, but if you want to compete, there are a variety of activities in which you can take part. You may want to join a Pony Club or a local chapter of the 4-H club. You can enter showing, jumping, and gymkhana competitions at local shows, and you might like to try dressage or hunter paces.

Riding clubs
Local riding clubs hold all kinds of events. If you become a member, you can take part and also find out about other equestrian activities going on in your area.

Endurance riding
If you take part in a long-distance endurance ride, you and your pony will need to be very fit. You may have to cover up to 50 miles (80km) a day. Arabian horses have good stamina and excel at this sport.

Vaulting
Vaulting is gymnastics on horseback and requires great athletic ability as well as riding skills. You can take part on your own or as part of a team, performing leaps and balancing feats with the horse on a lunge rein.

Braiding the mane

1 Dampen the mane, then, starting at the poll, divide it into same-size sections. Hold them in place with a rubber band tied loosely at the base.

2 Remove the rubber band, and tightly braid each section. Tie with rubber bands. Tie yarn over the rubber bands, leaving long ends.

3 Thread the yarn through a large needle and pull the ends up through the top of the braid, making a loop.

4 Roll up the braid by folding it in half again. Hold it in place by tying the yarn around it and knotting it. Cut off any excess yarn.

Getting ready for a show

Getting ready for a show is fun, but it is hard work and takes time to do it right. If the weather is warm, you can give your pony a bath, but if it is cold, just sponge your pony off. You must also groom your pony thoroughly. If you are braiding its mane and tail, do not wash them. It is difficult to braid a clean mane. You must make sure the tack is clean, too, so your pony will look its best.

Bands or sewn?
You can secure your pony's braids with special rubber bands made specifically for this purpose—they are tiny and available in different coat colors.

Making the most of your pony

Quarter marks

Make quarter marks on your pony's hindquarters by wetting the coat and brushing it in different angles. You can also use special stencils to make squares or diamonds. Use hairspray to make the marks last longer.

Make white tails and markings whiter by rubbing in cornstarch.

Trim hairy fetlocks and hairs under the jaw and on the muzzle.

Pull the mane after the pony has been exercised, when its skin

Pulling a mane

pores are open. Use a pulling comb to separate 3–4 long hairs from underneath, wrap them around the comb, then pull.

Hairdressing
If you end up with a few wisps of hair sticking out of the braids, use hair gel to smooth them down flat.

Braiding the forelock

Dampen the forelock and braid it in the same way as you have braided the mane, using the yarn to secure it in place. To reverse the braid, cross the strands of hair underneath, instead of over the top.

Trimming
Carefully trim any long hairs in the ears. Fold the sides of the ears together and trim off the hairs that stick out.

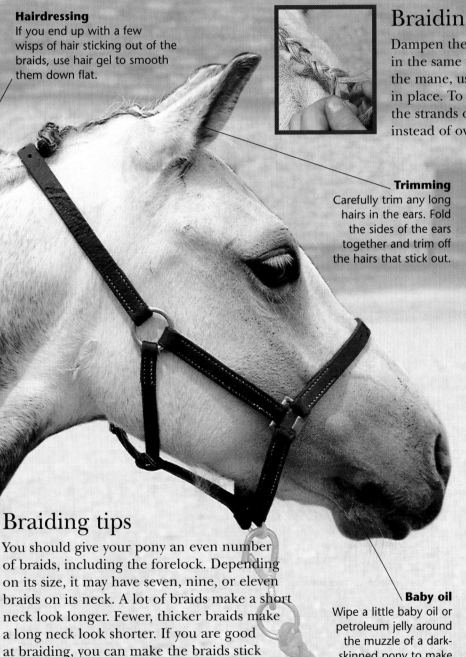

Braiding tips

You should give your pony an even number of braids, including the forelock. Depending on its size, it may have seven, nine, or eleven braids on its neck. A lot of braids make a short neck look longer. Fewer, thicker braids make a long neck look shorter. If you are good at braiding, you can make the braids stick up or lie flat to make the neck look wider or narrower.

Baby oil
Wipe a little baby oil or petroleum jelly around the muzzle of a dark-skinned pony to make it look clean and shiny.

Braiding the tail

Take long hairs from each side of the dock and braid them with hair from the center until you reach the end of the tailbone, then continue braiding without taking hair from the sides. Tie off the braid, fold it under, and secure with yarn.

Preparing for traveling

I f you compete in shows or riding club events, you will have to move your pony from place to place in a horse van or trailer. Most ponies do not mind traveling once they have gotten used to it. They learn to stand with their legs braced to absorb the movement and become good at balancing. But they do need to wear special equipment to protect them from accidental knocks and bumps.

Ready to go

This pony is prepared for a show and ready to load into the trailer. The blanket will help keep it clean, and the other equipment is so it will not get injured during its journey.

Bandaging the tail

A bandage keeps the top part of your pony's tail flat and neat. It also stops it from rubbing against the back wall of the van or trailer. You can use a tail guard instead of a bandage, or put one on top of the bandage.

1 Start to bandage the tail, leaving a corner of the bandage's end sticking out at the top.

2 After a few turns around the tail, fold the end down, and wind the bandage over it.

3 Bandage to the end of the dock, then work back up. Tie the strings with a bow.

4 Fold a layer of bandage over the bow to stop it from coming undone.

Removing a tail bandage

To take off a tail bandage, unfold the part over the tie, undo the strings, and slide the whole thing off, laying the tail hair flat as you do so. Roll up the bandage again, starting at the tie-strings end, with the strings on the inside.

Loading up

Walk your pony confidently up the middle of the ramp. Some ponies will walk straight into a trailer. If your pony is unsure, take a little time. Try lifting one of its front hooves onto the ramp, and try to have light coming in from the front end of the trailer.

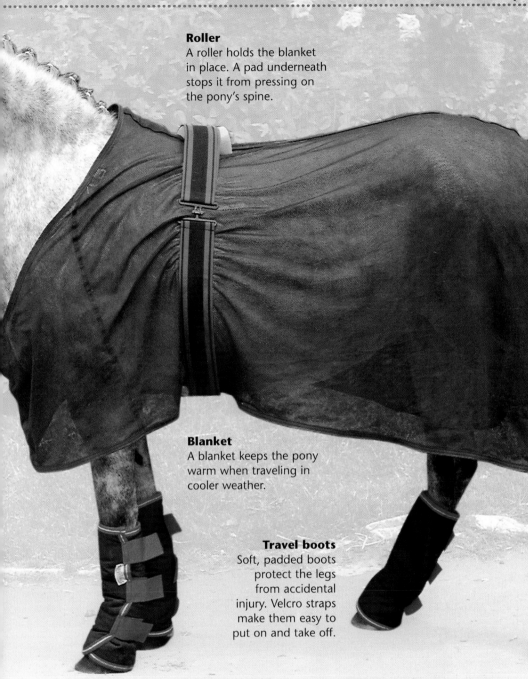

Roller
A roller holds the blanket in place. A pad underneath stops it from pressing on the pony's spine.

Clean tail
To keep the tail out of the way, put on a tail bandage, then fold up the tail and secure it with a rubber band.

Blanket
A blanket keeps the pony warm when traveling in cooler weather.

Travel boots
Soft, padded boots protect the legs from accidental injury. Velcro straps make them easy to put on and take off.

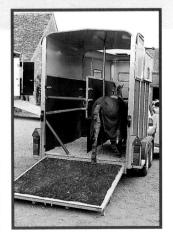

Tying up

Tie your pony in the trailer with a short lead rope so it cannot move its head around too much. Tie the rope to string, using a quick release knot. Some trailers and horse vans have crossties on each side of the horse's head, level with its chin, which clip to its halter.

Going to a show

Competing in a show is fun. After all the preparation, it is exciting to ride around the ring, looking your best and trying your hardest. In between classes, do not tear around, but let your pony rest in the shade. Give it a drink and some hay, or let it graze. It is great to win a ribbon, but do not blame your pony or get upset if you do not do it this time. There is always next time.

Unloading backward
If your pony needs to back out of a trailer, stand at its head and push it gently backward. Ask someone to stand by the ramp to guide it.

Unloading safely

Untie your pony before you take down the butt bar or butt chain. Lead it out forward if you can. When you go down the ramp, do not rush your pony. Some ramps are slippery and steep, and your pony could hurt itself if it goes too fast. Ask two friends to stand on either side of the ramp if you think your pony might try to jump off sideways.

Unloading forward
If the trailer has a side ramp, you can lead your pony out forward— you may have to lead it from the right side. Do not let it pull you.

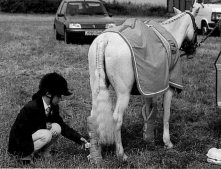

First things first
Tie up your pony, or ask someone to hold it while you take off its boots. Check it all over to see that it is all right after the journey.

Ready to jump
If you are entering a jumping event, it is a good idea to wear a body protector that meets safety standards.

Ready to show
Look as professional as you can for a showing class. It will give you confidence if you look your best.

Waiting safely

Leave your pony tied to a trailer only if you know it will not get upset. Fasten its lead rope to a piece of string so it can break free if it panics. Your pony will probably wait patiently if you hang up some hay for it.

The secretary

When you arrive at the show grounds, check in at the show secretary's tent or trailer. You can collect your number here and enter classes if you have not already done so. You can also find the results of classes here. The secretary will post them up on a noticeboard.

Sharing a pony

If you are sharing a pony with a friend, make sure you agree in advance which classes you will enter. It is fun to watch each other and help prepare for the classes. But do not ask your pony to do too much and exhaust it.

Fun and games

Gymkhanas and shows have all kinds of mounted games and races to try. Some are for teams, some for individuals. You need to be good at mounted games, be able to think and act quickly, and have an obedient and fast-moving pony. If you belong to a Pony Club, you could become a member of the mounted games team and compete around the country.

Handy tips

You need to be quick, fit, and athletic to do really well in mounted games.

Your pony must be fast, agile, and, above all, obedient—it is no use asking it to gallop if you cannot get it to stop or turn.

Practice makes perfect

No matter what games you enter, you need to practice for them. Training your pony until it responds to all your commands will make a big difference in competition. Practice going from a halt to a canter to a gallop, and changing gaits and direction at full speed. See how quickly you can mount and dismount, and learn how to vault on and off. You can also get used to leaning out of the saddle to pick things up.

Flag relay
This is a team game in which you have to gallop to a flag, lean over, and pick it up, then gallop back and hand it on to the next member of your team.

Barrel racing
A pony that can gallop and turn quickly without losing its balance is a great help in this type of bending race.

Vaulting on

Being able to vault onto your pony while it is moving saves a lot of time in games and races. It is easier if your pony is small and you have long legs! You have to run with your pony, holding the saddle, then spring up and swing yourself over.

Egg and spoon
You need a steady hand for this. The eggs are not real, but you still have to keep one on the spoon!

Tire race
You and a partner have to leap off your ponies, climb through a tire, and then get back on again.

Make a tower
You have to lean right out of the saddle to stack the plastic tubs without unbalancing your pony.

Potato race
Having picked up a potato and raced down the field, you then have to throw it into a bucket.

Show jumping classes

Show jumping is a popular riding sport. Most classes have a time limit, some are against the clock, where the fastest round with the least faults wins. You are penalized if your horse knocks down a fence, refuses a jump, runs out, or if you fall off. Three refusals or taking the wrong course means you are eliminated. If more than one person jumps a clean round, there is a "jump off." This means you will have to ride a shorter, timed course to decide the winner.

Walking the course

Before a show jumping class, all the competitors have a chance to walk the course. This gives you time to plan and memorize the route you will take. You can also look carefully at each jump and judge how many strides your pony will need to take between combination fences.

In the warm-up arena

The warm-up arena is an area, usually with one or two practice jumps, where you can warm up your pony before its class. Once the class has started, you will have to wait near the entrance to the ring for your number to be called.

Triple bars
Three bars, making a wide spread

Brush and rails
A spread highest in the center

Gate
A high, upright fence

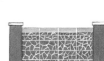

Wall
Made of "bricks" that fall off easily

Filler
A solid part below the poles

Upright poles
Poles right above each other

Double oxer
Brush between two sets of poles

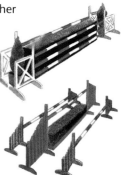

Hog's back
The highest pole is in the center

Types of jumps

Show jumps fall into four main categories: uprights, spreads, combinations, and water. Uprights are difficult for ponies to jump. Spread fences are easier because they are lower at the front. Combinations—jumps with only a stride or two between each fence—need good judgment from pony and rider. To clear water jumps, ponies have to stretch themselves out.

Thinking ahead

Throughout your round, it is important to keep a good position in the saddle. Drive your pony forward confidently as you jump, and look ahead to the next fence.

Saving time

It is important to memorize the course before you enter the ring so that as you land from each jump, you can be thinking about the next one. Against the clock, you can save precious seconds by taking the shortest route between fences.

Clean round

Do not rush around the ring—your pony will lose balance and hit fences.

Push your pony firmly toward each fence. If it feels you hesitate, it may refuse.

If you feel your pony may refuse, give it a sharp tap with your crop behind the girth.

Do not hit your pony if it knocks a fence—just try to approach it better next time.

Showing and dressage tests

To compete in the show ring and dressage arena you need a well-trained horse or pony, and both of you must be clean and professional. In the show ring, a pony is judged on its conformation—its shape and proportions—its gaits, and its behavior. You will have to ride at a walk, trot, and canter on both reins; walk and trot your pony in hand; and sometimes do an individual show.

Showing in hand

When you are lined up in the ring, you will be asked to take off your pony's saddle so that the judge can inspect the pony. Then you will have to walk and trot your pony in hand so the judge can check that it moves straight.

Individual show

An individual show is a chance to show off your pony's gaits. Most people ride circles at trot and canter on both reins, or combine them to form a figure eight. At the end of your time, finish with a good, square halt.

Before the test

Before doing a dressage test, warm up a pony thoroughly to get it settled and working at its best. Some horses and ponies need more work than others, so give yourself plenty of time.

Riding the test

Concentrate and keep calm when riding in the dressage arena. The judges mark the test and write their comments on a score sheet. You will be given the sheet—it is a useful pointer to your strengths and weaknesses.

Dressage hints and tips

Check that your clothes and tack meet the requirements of the competition.

Make sure that you and your pony are immaculately clean and well groomed. It is important to make a good first impression on the judges.

Ask someone to call out each bit of the test as you practice, to help you remember it.

Make up rhymes to help you memorize the test.

Practice until you and your pony can carry out the test's requirements perfectly.

Aim for the top

Some riders and their horses specialize in dressage. This is Isabell Werth on Gigolo doing an extended trot at the World Equestrian Games in 1998. A great deal of training and effort lies behind the tests performed by top-class horses and riders.

Cross-country

Hedge

Ski jump

Log

Tires

Rails

On a cross-country course, there are solid fences with long spaces in between. Both you and your pony need to be strong and brave. You will pick up penalty points for every mistake you make, such as refusing, jumping the wrong part of a fence, going the wrong way, falling off, or going over the time limit. The fences carry red and white flags. You must jump between them with the red on your right and the white on your left. You may have the choice between an easier, slower route or a faster, more difficult one.

Hunter paces

Cross-country jumping competitions are called hunter paces. There are paces for both horses and ponies. Courses often take you through fields and woodland, and you may have to open and close a gate. There is usually a set time in which you must try to finish one section or the whole course.

Types of fences

Cross-country fences are based on obstacles you might meet if you were riding through the countryside, such as rails, hedges, logs, walls, ditches, banks, and water. They are solid and do not give way if hit. They may be placed so that you have to jump them going up or down hills.

Walking the course

You are allowed to walk around a cross-country course before you ride it. This allows you to look at the fences and work out the best way to approach them. Check the ground on the approach and landing, and look out for things that might spook your pony, so that you are prepared.

Horse trials

In horse trials, you have to do dressage, cross-country, and show jumping. These are the supreme test of horse and rider. Precision and training is needed for the dressage; endurance, speed, and boldness for the cross-country; and suppleness and obedience for the show jumping. Experienced riders take part in events that last two or three days.

Steeplechase

Two- and three-day events include a steeplechase phase—about 12 fences over a distance of about 2.2 miles (3.6km). The course has to be ridden at around 25 mph (41km/h), which means a horse has to perform like a racehorse. At large events, competitors also have to ride along sections of roads and tracks, both before and after the steeplechase.

Gallop—the fastest gait

Glossary

The horse and pony world has a language of its own, and you might not understand all the words you read and hear. This list explains what some of those words mean.

aids The signals that a rider uses to tell a horse what to do. Natural aids are the rider's lower legs, **seat**, hands, and voice. Artificial aids include crops and spurs.

bit The part of a bridle that goes in a horse's mouth—usually made of steel—to which the reins are attached for control.

blaze A wide, white mark down the front of a horse's face.

breastplate A strap that fastens to the front of the saddle. It prevents the saddle from slipping backward.

cantle The back of a saddle.

cavesson a) A type of noseband. b) A halter with swivel rings to which a lunge rein is attached.

changing the rein Changing the direction you are riding in the ring.

chaps Leather or suede leggings worn over pants to protect a rider's legs. They may be full-length, or half chaps up to the knee.

clipping Removing a horse's winter coat so it sweats less when working.

collection A shortening of the horse's frame, so it pushes off its haunches, making the stride shorter and bouncier.

colt A male horse under four years old.

concentrated feed Pellets or mixed feeds, like sweet feeds, that are fed in smaller quantities, as opposed to bulk feeds such as grass or hay.

conformation The overall shape and proportions of a horse or pony.

contact A slight tension from your pony's mouth felt through the reins.

cross cantering Cantering with one leg leading in front and the opposite leg leading behind.

curry comb A plastic, rubber, or metal brush. The curry comb is used in a circular motion and is the first step when grooming to remove mud and loose hairs.

diagonal When a horse trots, its legs move in diagonal pairs: right front and left back, left front and right back. A **posting** rider rises on one **stride** and sits on the other. They are on the right or the left diagonal, depending on which front leg they rise to.

dismount To get off a horse or pony.

double bridle A bridle with two bits, used mostly for dressage and showing.

dressage (The French word for "training.") The advanced training of a horse to perform precise movements in response to barely visible signals from the rider.

extension A lengthening of a horse's frame, so it moves faster with longer, lower strides. The opposite of **collection**.

feather The long hair that grows around the **fetlocks** of draft horses and some ponies.

fetlocks The joints on the lower part of a horse's legs just above the hooves.

filly A female horse under four years old.

flash noseband A noseband that fastens under the bit, preventing a horse from opening its mouth to avoid pressure on the bit.

flying change Changing the **lead** when the horse has all four hooves off the ground while cantering.

foal A horse or pony under the age of one year old.

forelock The part of the mane that hangs between a horse's ears and covers the forehead.

Gymkhana game

frog The V-shaped structure in the sole of a horse's hoof.

gait The manner in which a horse or pony moves. The natural gaits are walk, trot, canter, and gallop. Other gaits can be taught.

gelding A castrated male horse or pony. It is unable to breed.

girth The broad strap that goes around a horse's belly to hold the saddle in place.

gymkhana Mounted games and races, usually performed as part of a show.

hackamore A bridle without a bit.

half seat position The position to take when galloping—leaning forward with your bottom out of the saddle, taking your weight on your knees and lower legs.

hands The units of measurement used for a horse's height. One hand equals 4 in. (10cm).

hindquarters The area of a horse behind the saddle, including its croup, loins, and hind legs.

in hand A class in a show in which the riders lead their horses while on foot.

jump off An extra round or rounds, used to decide

Saddle pad

Dapple-gray horse   Shetland Pony mare with foal

Riding crops

the winner in show jumping when two or more competitors have the same score.

jumping position Also called forward seat. Lean forward over the pony's neck and push your arms forward so your elbows are slightly in front of your body. This position makes it easier for the pony to jump, because the rider does not bounce around on its back.

Rider in casual gear

lead The front leg that reaches out the farthest and strikes the ground first during a canter.

leading file The front horse and rider of a group.

leg up An easy way of getting on a horse. A helper holds a rider's left leg and helps them spring up into the saddle.

loose box A separate stall in which a horse is free to move around.

lungeing Exercising a riderless horse on a long rein attached to a special halter. The horse is asked to walk, trot, and canter in a circle in both directions.

mare A female horse or pony four years old or older.

near side The left side of a horse or pony.

neck strap A strap that fastens around a horse's neck for a rider to hold on to while jumping, for example.

novice An inexperienced rider or horse.

off side The right side of a horse or pony.

on the bit When a horse or pony is balanced between the rider's hands and legs and is pushed into a soft **contact** with the bit. This allows maximum control and a true feeling of the pony's movements.

pace A specific gait in which a horse moves both legs on one side together.

Palomino A horse or pony with a golden coat and a white mane and tail.

Pelham A type of **bit** with two sets of reins, or one set with a rein adapter, and a curb chain.

points a) The visible features of a horse. b) Areas on a horse that are described as part of its color. A horse with "black points" has a black mane, tail, and lower legs.

pommel The front part of a saddle.

posting Rising from the saddle during a recurring diagonal in a trot.

quarter marks Patterns made on the **hindquarters** by brushing against the lie of the coat with a damp brush.

quick release knot A knot used to tie up a horse. Pulling the end of the rope releases the knot instantly.

roller A broad band that fastens around a horse's belly to hold a blanket in place.

saddle pad A pad used under the saddle to absorb the horse's sweat and also to prevent the saddle from chafing the horse's back.

seat a) A rider's position in the saddle. b) The part of the saddle on which a rider sits.

seatbones The two bones of your bottom, which you use to follow the motion of the horse and feel its stride.

skipping out Collecting droppings from a stall in a bucket.

sound A horse in good health and condition, which does not have any signs of lameness or breathing problems.

spread fence A wide fence with the back part higher than the front.

square a) The rider's weight is distributed evenly in the seat. b) The horse stands with its front and hind hooves parallel and its weight evenly balanced.

stallion A male horse or pony, four years old, or older, used for breeding.

stride The distance traveled by a horse's hoof between two successive impacts with the ground.

surcingle a) A strap attached to a blanket, used to fasten it around a horse's belly. b) A strap that goes over a racing saddle for extra security.

tack A horse's riding outfit of saddle and bridle; also

a halter and other accessories.

Thoroughbred The fastest breed of horse.

training on the flat Training "on the ground," learning simple dressage movements, as opposed to training over fences, or is learning to jump.

transition The change from one **gait** to another. An upward transition is from a slower to a faster gait; a downward transition is from a faster to a slower gait.

turn out To let a horse loose in a pasture.

vaulting a) Jumping up onto a horse without using the stirrups. b) Gymnastics on horseback.

warm-up arena A small ring outside of the main show ring, where competitors gather before a class.

wings The extensions at the sides of a jump.

withers The bony ridge at the base of a horse's neck.

worming Giving medicine to kill parasitic worms inside a horse's intestines.

Index

HORSE AND PONY WEBSITES

- www.ponyclub.org (official Pony Club site)
- www.ilph.org (International League for the Protection of Horses)
- www.ahsa.org (American Horse Shows Association)
- www.newrider.com (advice and information for new riders)
- www.nhjc.org (National Hunter/Jumper Council)
- www.equiworld.net (international horse and pony information)
- www.aqha.com (American Quarter Horse Association)
- www.youngrider.com (links to other horse and pony sites)

Kingfisher would like to thank:
The Hutton family and Patricia Curtis, as well as the models: Alison Jane Berman, Parker Dunn, Theo Freyne, Emma Harford, Brian Hutton, Charlie Hutton, Pippa Hutton, Pete Jenkins (equine dentist), Eric Lin, Lucy Miller (advanced riding), Charlotte Nagle, Jay Rathore, Nicola Ridley, Ignacio Romero Torres, Victoria Taylor, Sophie Thomas, Ayako Watanabe, and Sawako Yoshii. Also, many thanks to Lesley Ward.

Jacket photographs: Only Horses Picture Agency; gettyone Stone/Art Wolfe